IN A WEEK

Martin Manser

WITHDRAWN

The *Teach Yourself* series has been trusted around the world
for over 60 years. This series of 'In A Week' business books is
designed to help people at all levels and around the world to
further their careers. Learn in a week, what the experts learn in
a lifetime.

Martin Manser's major management experience has been in managing people and projects, including leading a team of nearly 100 people to manage one of the few 20th-century study Bibles (*The Thematic Reference Bible*, Hodder and Stoughton, 1996) to be originated in the UK. He has also led teams to manage the award-winning *Collins Bible Companion* (Harper Collins, 2009) and the best-selling *Macmillan Student's Dictionary* (Macmillan, 2nd edition, 1996). He is a Language Trainer and Consultant with national and international companies and organizations, leading courses on project management and business skills and communications.

www.martinmanser.com

Acknowledgements

I wish to thank my daughter Hannah Murphy for her comments on early drafts of this text and Linda Eley for her careful typing of my manuscript.

Martin Manser

Teach® Yourself

Introducing Management

Martin Manser

www.inaweek.co.uk

Hodder Education

338 Euston Road, London NW1 3BH

Hodder Education is an Hachette UK company

First published in UK 2012 by Hodder Education

First published in US 2012 by The McGraw-Hill Companies, Inc.

Copyright © 2012 Martin Manser

British Library Cataloguing in Publication Data: a catalogue record for this title is available from the British Library.

Library of Congress Catalog Card Number: on file.

10 9 8 7 6 5 4 3 2 1

www.hoddereducation.co.uk

Typeset by Cenveo Publisher Services.

Printed in Great Britain by CPI Cox & Wyman, Reading.

Contents

Introduction

Congratulations! You've made it! Your bosses have seen your potential. They have noticed your hard work and the skills you have and have promoted you to a manager.

How do you feel? Excited? Thrilled at the prospect of showing your abilities and skills even more? Exhilarated at the opportunities that will open up for you to shine even further? Perhaps a little overawed at some of the responsibilities that will come your way? Concerned, even anxious, about some of the burdens that the management role will bring?

I've written this short book to guide you through what can feel like the maze of tasks of a manager. I have tried to keep it simple by explaining principles, with case studies giving examples of how – and sometimes how not – to manage.

Where do you start? How do you see your way more clearly? I've broken down the subject into easy steps:

Sunday Becoming a manager: what the changes will mean to you in your new role

Monday Managing people: recruiting, developing and motivating your staff

Tuesday Managing a team: encouraging members of your team to work well together

Wednesday Managing your work: setting goals, managing systems and procedures, solving problems and making decisions

Thursday Communicating effectively: keeping lines of communication clear through good listening skills, effective use of email and telephone and holding better meetings

Friday Managing a project: working out – and keeping to – aims, outputs, costs and schedules

Saturday Managing yourself: being aware of yourself, becoming organized and making good use of your time

Each day of the week covers a different key area and the material is structured by beginning with an introduction that gives a 'heads-up' as to what the day is about. Then comes the main material, which explains the key lessons to be learnt by clarifying important principles that are backed up by case studies and quotations. Each day concludes with a summary, next steps and multiple-choice questions, to reinforce the key learning points.

There are many other books on management available that will explain theories of management, but I've written this book to guide you reliably through the basics. I'm writing from a background of managing people, teams and projects over 30 years, including over ten years' experience of writing about and training colleagues in such subjects. During my working life, I've made quite a few mistakes but also seen many successes.

Managing is hard work but an exciting experience and I wish you well in this adventure.

Martin Manser

SUNDAY

Becoming a manager

Today we're going to look at:

- what managing is
- some challenges you will face
- the differences between managing and leading
- the qualities of a successful manager.

Dictionaries give different definitions of the verb 'manage'. Our main concern is with *organizing other workers and making decisions about how a business or department is run*. In practice this will mean that you usually *tell other people what to do rather than doing it yourself*. The italic text shows the crucial differences between what you have done up to now and what you will do now you are a manager. You will:

- organize other workers
- make decisions about how a business or department is run
- tell other people what to do rather than doing it yourself.

You are not uninformed, however. You will have had experience. In the past, you will have been organized by your boss who made decisions about how the business or department should be run. So you have thoughts about how well or badly that management was undertaken. Also, be assured that your bosses have identified potential in you that can be developed successfully.

What is managing?

We can usefully divide managing into separate tasks:

- **Plan**: know your goals and work out how to achieve them.
- **Organize**: do what is necessary to make the plan happen. Bring structure and make arrangements. Allocate the necessary resources to your team. Assign work to your team members; if necessary, recruit or train your team. Co-ordinate with others. <u>Delegate work, responsibility and authority</u>. Work efficiently, with minimal waste of time, money and other resources.
- **Lead**: motivate, encourage and, above all, communicate with members of your team to show them they are valued and get the best out of them so they work effectively.
- **Control**: not in the control-freak or manipulative sense, but being direct, making decisions about how to work most effectively to see that your goals are met. Monitor actual timings and costs against planned goals and take steps to ensure that the agreed outputs, standards and so on are met.

MR. ORGANISED

Looking at the four points above, think which of these come naturally to you and which you will need to work harder at to cultivate. Think about your new role and analyse it in terms of each of these task points.

What goals will you need to *plan*? How will you *organize* the necessary resources to achieve that plan? How will you *lead* – motivate – your team members to get the best out of them, *controlling* and giving direction to make decisions to see that your goals are met?

Challenges you face

Challenges you face as a manager may include:

- hiring the right staff
- making the most of scarce financial resources
- training your staff
- managing difficult members of your team
- motivating and encouraging your team
- communicating well with your team
- making better use of your time
- managing budgets
- managing projects
- managing yourself better.

We will deal with these, and more, in this text.

Becoming a manager

When Karen first became a manager, she was in charge of people who had previously been on the same level as her. She was once one of them but was now senior to them.

She had lots of ideas when she became team leader, such as introducing new daily briefings and performance targets. However, rather than implementing these changes gradually, she tried to introduce them all at once. Unfortunately, the team did not cope well with this and their attitude to her became negative. She decided to have one-to-one meetings with each colleague to find out their thoughts on the changes and hear their suggestions. These sessions proved to be opportunities for them to understand that the changes were for the good of the team, and gradually Karen was able to introduce all the changes successfully.

Managing and leading

What is the difference between managing and leading? Roughly speaking, managing is turning leadership into action.

Let's consider this in more detail. Leaders set a particular course: 'We're going to expand into the Chinese market.' Managers put that into action, for example: 'We're going to understand the culture, build a base, recruit staff there and implement a whole range of other activities to make the basic idea of "expanding into the Chinese market" a reality.'

So leaders set the overall direction and give vision; managers work out the detail in terms of organizing people, planning and budgeting. You will probably have agreed with this last sentence, but notice that it includes a crucial aspect: that of emotions. Leaders appeal to the emotions to set a course of change, wanting to inspire people to follow a vision. Managers, in contrast it seems, have the less exciting task of ensuring that the work, in all its detail, is completed.

In practice, however, the distinction between 'leader' and 'manager' may not be so clear-cut. Your role may be 'team leader' and your responsibilities will concentrate on the detailed tasks, systems and processes to ensure that the work is completed. You will also, however, need leadership skills to motivate the members of your team to achieve these goals.

Proving your capabilities

Louise first joined the help desk at the hospital's IT department via an agency. She'd always been interested in computers and was good at explaining things to other people in a pleasant and clear manner. She was quickly taken on to the permanent staff at the hospital.

Colleagues gradually noticed that she was quick to pick up knowledge and that she had good organizational skills – from arranging rotas to organizing the staff's Christmas meal. She also often deputized for the team leader when he was unavailable. She was promoted to acting team

SUNDAY
MONDAY
TUESDAY
WEDNESDAY
THURSDAY
FRIDAY
SATURDAY

leader when the team leader was on sick leave. Louise proved her capabilities so well that when the team leader's job became vacant she applied and was offered this role. Her work skills, linked with her dedication, hard work and commitment to the role over a period of years meant that she was an ideal person to manage the team.

Qualities of a successful manager

What kind of a person makes a successful manager?

- Someone who is self-motivated – a good manager will have initiative and determination; he or she will not need external persuasion in order to work.
- Someone with good directional and organizational skills to organize people, processes and resources.
- Someone who is able to plan ahead and set clear goals.
- Someone who is focused on the important aims of achieving goals and increasing performance.
- Someone who has vision and is able to inspire others by their words and their example.
- Someone who is proactive in looking ahead, rather than reacting to changes as they happen.
- An effective communicator, able to communicate clearly in spoken and written forms (e.g. emails, reports).
- Someone who is able to think strategically, taking a view above the detailed.

9

- Someone who is good with finances, setting budgets and establishing systems that monitor and control expenditure.
- Someone who is good at analysing information, both in words and numbers, text and financial data, at home with both text documents and spreadsheets.
- Someone who is decisive, with the ability to take the initiative and make decisions. Sometimes even making the wrong decision can be better than making no decision at all!
- Someone with good interpersonal skills: open and approachable, trustworthy. Someone who respects others.
- Someone who is able to motivate others, coaching, supporting and facilitating their staff.
- Someone who is good at networking with others to develop trusted relationships.
- Someone who is able to delegate to members of their team.
- Someone who is able to work well under pressure.
- A good team player – one who works well, establishing clear roles and encouraging personal responsibility.
- Someone who is able to recruit (and retain!) good staff.
- Someone who is able to take control, building on previous successes to make things happen.
- Someone who is confident and optimistic – able to boost staff morale and encourage them to see challenges in a positive light.

- Someone who is effective at using time well, especially doing things right the first time.

- Someone who is committed and persistent in completing tasks reliably.
- Someone who is adaptable, able to deal with people well and solve problems creatively.
- Someone who is good at managing themselves, being aware of their own strengths and areas that need development.
- Someone with honesty and integrity, who deals with all staff fairly.

Tip

A few years ago I went to a day's course on leadership at which various skills (e.g. giving vision and direction, having courage, being able to inspire others) were stressed. The final comment of the day has stuck with me, however: 'Most importantly, if you had to choose between skills and integrity, choose integrity.'

The function which distinguishes the manager above all others is his educational one. The one contribution he is uniquely expected to make is to give others vision and ability to perform. It is vision and moral responsibility that, in the last analysis, define the manager.

Peter F. Drucker (1909–2005), US management expert

Back to the shop floor

As Managing Director, Joe felt he needed to 'get back to the shop floor' and find out what his staff really thought of his organization. So he sat alongside members of staff for several days, listening to their concerns. They didn't feel their work was valued, and communications from 'them' (senior management) were thought to be very poor. At the end of the week, Joe was able to take these valuable lessons back to his role as MD and begin to change the company's ethos and practices.

Summary

Today, we've begun to consider:

- what a manager is and does
- key aspects of being a manager
  - directing, planning and organizing work
  - giving instructions to workers
  - making decisions about aims and work
  - supervising and motivating staff
- the differences between being a manager and a leader
  - leaders set the overall direction and vision; managers turn that vision into action
  - in practice, the distinction between manager and leader may not be clear-cut
- the qualities that make a successful manager.

Next steps

1 Summarize your role in 10 to 15 words.

2 List the three main functions of your role.

3 Which of these three comes most easily to you?

4 Which of these three do you consider most difficult? Why? What will you do about it?

5 To what extent are you also a leader in your role as manager?

6 Consider which qualities of a successful manager you need to cultivate.

Questions (answers at the back)

1. A manager is:
   a) a successful person ☐
   b) someone who works hard ☐
   c) someone who organizes work and gives instructions to colleagues ☐
   d) someone who bosses others around. ☐

2. Managing is:
   a) turning action into leadership ☐
   b) setting a vision ☐
   c) just about coping with difficulties ☐
   d) turning leadership into action. ☐

3. As team leader, your role is:
   a) to give orders to the team ☐
   b) to manage the team ☐
   c) to allow the team to do what they want ☐
   d) to give days off to the team. ☐

4. A manager needs to be:
   a) poorly motivated ☐
   b) self-motivated and good at motivating others ☐
   c) self-motivated ☐
   d) good at motivating others. ☐

5. A manager needs to:
   a) be good at organizing ☐
   b) be poor at organizing ☐
   c) not care about organizing. ☐
   d) Sorry, what is organizing? ☐

6. A manager needs to:
   a) be confused about the goals they want to achieve ☐
   b) not care about the goals they want to achieve ☐
   c) be clear about the goals they want to achieve ☐
   d) change their mind about the goals they want to achieve. ☐

7. A manager needs to:
   a) be totally absorbed by basic financial information ☐
   b) be uninterested in basic financial information ☐
   c) not care about basic financial information ☐
   d) be able to understand basic financial information. ☐

8. A good manager should:
   a) be proactive not reactive ☐
   b) be reactive not proactive ☐
   c) know the difference between proactive and reactive ☐
   d) not understand the difference between proactive and reactive. ☐

9. A good manager should:
   a) make decisions, but change the decision later ☐
   b) never make any decisions at all ☐
   c) be decisive, making clear decisions ☐
   d) be hesitant, afraid to make decisions. ☐

10. In the final analysis, which is more important in a manager: skills or integrity?
    a) both ☐
    b) neither ☐
    c) skills ☐
    d) integrity. ☐

G/10   60 %

MONDAY

Managing people

So you're a new manager. Who will you manage? People are not things like machines, computers or processes – they are individuals, with different personalities. Some colleagues are keen to work, others lack motivation. Some colleagues are quick, others are slow; each has their own approach and style of working. How will you cope? How will you get the best out of them?

Today we look at:

- recruiting the right staff: the different steps you need to take
- motivating your staff: some useful hints, tips and techniques
- performance management, to evaluate colleagues' work
- developing your staff so that they gain new skills and abilities.

Each of these is vital: you want the best staff and you want them to reach their full potential. You need to build good relationships with them. This is about believing in your colleagues, having confidence in them.

Recruiting the right staff

It is difficult to find the colleagues you want. We joke, 'You can't get the staff these days', but it may be true. How do you find the best staff? Here's part of the secret: you need to know the kind of people you want.

Work out a timetable for the various different elements of the task, beginning at the end – in other words, the ideal date when you want the person to start. Working from where you are now, include time for: agreeing job description, person specification and method of application; advertising the post; receiving applications; dealing with references; shortlisting; interviewing; offering the job; applicant accepting offer; signing of contract.

Defining the job and the person

You need to start with a **job description**, which will state:

- what the purpose of the job is
- what the main responsibilities of the job are
- who the person will be responsible to.

Don't just use the standard job description that may be on your computer or filed in the Human Resources (HR) Department; now is a good time to review it and to refine the tasks and requirements of that position.

You will also need to define the skills, qualifications and experience the person will need. You will do this in a **person specification**. Some of these will be essential, others desirable. For example, to be a team leader at a Customer Services help desk, it is essential to have previous experience of working in Customer Services. Are you looking for a good team player or a lone ranger who is better at working by themselves? Are you looking for someone who can plan ahead? Someone who works well with spreadsheets?

Advertising the job

So, you've agreed and written up the job description and a person specification, now you need to move the recruitment process forward. Your Human Resources Department will help you with this. Advertise the post internally (e.g. on your organization's website) and externally. Advertise on the internet and intranet, in internal news bulletins and newspapers. If appropriate, go to an agency.

You will need to decide how to handle applications: whether candidates should fill in an application form (physically or online) or send a covering letter explaining why they think they are suitable for the job, accompanied by their CV.

You will also need to decide whether to ask for references and, if so, when (before or after the interview).

When you receive applications, you will then, with colleagues, shortlist possible candidates according to the objective criteria you decided in the job description and person specification. Note why you are not pursuing certain people and their applications in case this is queried later. Consider how many people you want to interview. Is ten too many?

Interviewing staff

The key point of interviews lies in the preparation. Be clear on the time and place of the interview, and give candidates sufficient advance notice (e.g. allow a week between shortlisting and the actual interview). On the day, allow enough time for the interviews themselves and time between interviews for the interviewers to make notes and confer before the next interview.

Think through what you want. Will candidates be required to give a presentation or take a test? If you want them to give a presentation, will a projector and laptop be available? And will they be required to bring some proof of identity or examination certificates?

Decide who will carry out the interviews. Do you require another person or possibly another two? Depending on how many candidates you are interviewing, is it better to do the interviews in a block, say over two days, so candidates are fresh in your mind. This may not always be possible, which is why it is vital to make notes.

Prepare the interview room, making sure it is clean and that water is available for candidates and pens and paper for interviewers.

Work hard at phrasing your questions. Apply the agreed criteria in the job description and the person specification in the interview process. It is important that each candidate is treated equally in the interviews: they should all be asked the same questions in the same order. Avoid closed questions that can be answered by a simple yes or no. Instead ask open questions. You could start with a general question such as, 'Tell us why you think you can fulfil this role'. Your aim is to enable the candidates to talk about themselves, their previous experience and how they could fill the job you are interviewing for. Check that you are clear on basic matters such as pay scales.

There are certain questions that you cannot ask, by law, such as a person's sexual orientation or their marital status. Your HR department will advise you on this.

Make sure you have discussed with the other interviewers when you will be able to let candidates know whether you are offering them the job.

A model interview

Harry welcomed the candidates to the day's interviews and tried to help them relax by making small talk. At the beginning of each interview, Harry started by explaining to each candidate the role and purpose of the job, the type of person the company was looking for and how the interview would proceed.

There were three interviewers on the panel and each asked the candidate the questions they had agreed in advance, with one or two supplementary questions to clarify their answers. They discussed the candidate's previous experience, what challenges they had faced in their previous job, their strengths and where they felt they could develop their performance. They allowed time for the candidate to ask questions and provide any other information they thought would be relevant. During the interview, each interviewer wrote many notes, which later formed the basis of their evaluation, discussion and decision on the best person for the job.

Evaluation

You will have all the information before you and you need to be as objective as possible in deciding to whom you should offer the job. Consider the facts as you have them from the candidates' applications, interviews and any references. Don't let yourself be persuaded by a person's attractive appearance or warm personality; you are interested in their ability to perform the job.

Offering the job and induction

Your HR department will guide you on your organization's practice regarding job offers/letters of appointment and contracts. You should also inform other candidates that they were not successful.

If the new colleague has come from outside the organization, then make sure you have a good induction programme to show them how your organization works, and to make them feel at home and integrated into their new workplace. It's not only about big ideas such as the ethos of your organization and its health and safety policy, but also about the small details of how to apply for holidays and who to contact if they are ill.

Staff Handbook

A typical Employees' Handbook (also called Employee Handbook, Employee Manual, Staff Handbook) contains sections on:

absence

appeal procedure

bullying

confidentiality

contract of employment

data protection

disciplinary procedure

equal opportunity and non-discrimination policies

expenses guidelines

flexible working procedures and conditions

grievance procedures

health, safety and fire

holiday entitlement

hours of work

maternity and paternity leave

notice to terminate employment

payments, including annual review

pension scheme arrangements

personal development

probationary period

redundancy policy

retirement age

sickness and sick pay procedures.

Motivating your staff

It's Thursday afternoon and members of your team have, it seems, stopped working and are discussing tonight's football match. You try to get them back to work, but fail. And it's like that all too often. How can you motivate your staff? Or you may be coming to the end of a long project. As Team Leader, you should be aware of the motivations and emotions of members of your team. Colleagues are probably tired and their levels of energy and enthusiasm may be beginning to wane. How do you encourage them?

Someone who is well motivated is positive, does their job well and enthusiastically and wants more responsibility. Such a person can boost the morale of colleagues and help them work well. On the other hand, someone who is poorly motivated will not seem to care about their work. They may turn up late and complain about small details. Such a person can have a negative effect on other colleagues.

Here are some tips to motivate staff:

- Show that you value them. Listen to them. Be available for them to bring their concerns to you. Understand them. Try to find out 'what makes them tick'. Talk *to* them, not *at* them. Find out what interests them outside work.
- Show that you value their work. Imagine a worker who produces a small part in a large machine without knowing what the large machine is for. He would feel more fulfilled if he knew the broader picture – and it will be the same with your team.
- Ensure their work is interesting and challenging. No one likes boring, repetitive tasks. Make sure your colleagues' work contains at least some interesting tasks that will stretch them.
- Communicate with them, both formally in meetings but also informally as you walk down the corridor for a coffee break. By 'communicating' I mean speaking, not emailing or texting! (See **Thursday** for more on communicating.)
- In group meetings, encourage team members, constantly affirming the team's commitment to reach the goal.

21

- Delegate more of your own work (see also **Tuesday**). Delegate whole tasks where possible. I once delegated three different aspects of the same task to three different people, and all felt frustrated and unfulfilled at the thirds they were given.
- Delegate work clearly (see also **Tuesday**). Do colleagues know exactly what is expected of them? Vague and unclear instructions not only demotivate colleagues but also waste time.
- Encourage unco-operative colleagues to try a new system if they are reluctant to follow it. Or even ask them if they could suggest new ways of solving a problem.
- Know colleagues' strengths and weaknesses. Try as far as possible to make sure they are 'round pegs in round holes' rather than 'square pegs in round holes'. This may be difficult, as there will always be aspects of work (perhaps unexciting administrative tasks) that it seems no one wants to do.
- Encourage your colleagues to focus on the goal and recognize their progress on the way. When I go on a long-haul flight, I keep an eye on our progress. For example, I work out on a 13-hour flight what percentage of the journey I have covered after, say, 45 minutes (6 per cent), 1.5 hours (12 per cent) and so on. Focusing on the end goal, dividing up the overall journey time and measuring progress in a concrete way helps me feel I am on my way to reaching that goal.
- Take one step at a time. Our proverbs tell us, 'Rome wasn't built in a day', 'The journey of 1,000 miles begins with a first step'. Sometimes the longest journey can be the first step.
- Focus on specific, measurable and realistic goals (see SMART goals below), not on vague ideas.
- Try to remain positive even when doing a structured task. That structured task is a significant part of a bigger picture.
- Offer coaching and opportunities for development to all colleagues in areas where they need further help (see below).
- Recognize colleagues' achievements. Even saying, 'Thank you, you did that well,' is an acknowledgement of gratitude.

Publicly affirm and recognize colleagues' achievements; praise their work in front of others. Bring in food or buy each of them little treats, such as chocolate. Issue certificates for achievements: it's amazing how competitive colleagues can be for a certificate.

- If you have come to the end of a project, celebrate that fact by all going out for a meal.
- Involve colleagues in decision making and setting budgets. If your company or organization is undergoing a period of change, then involve your colleagues at an earlier, rather than a later, stage. They will then feel valued.
- Encourage colleagues to make positive suggestions as to how to work more effectively.
- Ask a trusted colleague to come with you to a meeting of other managers. Let them accompany you for a few meetings and then gradually delegate some of the responsibilities to them.
- Recognize that on some days you will not feel motivated. You cannot feel fully inspired all the time. On days when I don't feel at all motivated, I really have to push myself to make an effort and often – but not always! – a sense of fulfilment comes.
- Overcome negative feelings – 'feel the fear and do it anyway'.

Performance management

Most organizations have certain procedures in place to consider colleagues' performance. Such procedures, usually included in your Employees' Handbook are commonly known as 'performance management', but other terms such as 'performance appraisal' and 'coaching development' are also used.

Appraisals

In an appraisal, a manager meets regularly (e.g. yearly or twice yearly) with a member of their team to discuss that colleague's work. In particular, the manager will consider the following:

- The colleague's performance since the last review. What has gone well? What evidence can you show to demonstrate this? Have the goals that were set then been fulfilled? If not, why not?
- Possible future development needs. In what areas would they benefit from training, or do they need support? What skills do they need to develop to enable them to progress in their career? You may gather information about their work from other individuals they work with, such as fellow team members, co-workers, subordinates, customers. When feedback is given from a range of people at different levels in the hierarchy it is known as 360-degree appraisal, indicating the all-round picture this will give of an individual.

The general tone of an appraisal is important. I was taught to follow the 'high-low-high' method – begin and end with praise and commendation and sandwich in between discussion of an area that has not gone well. A key aim is to get the appraisee to do most of the talking. Listen to your colleague's explanation of an area of their work where they are performing less well – there may be mitigating factors that have affected their work. Remain fair, positive and constructive and tackle weak performance by identifying causes and pursuing appropriate remedies. (Your company will have procedures in place for instances where required standards have not been met on a long-term basis.)

An appraisal should end by setting <u>objectives</u>. These objectives should be SMART:

S: Specific – defining the desired results

M: Measurable – quantifiable so that you know whether the objectives have been reached

A: Agreed by both the manager and the person being appraised

R: Realistic – objectives should be achievable but not too easy; should develop and challenge ('stretch') the colleague's resources and skills

T: Timed – giving a date for completion.

Making appraisals less difficult

Jack and his colleagues hated the yearly appraisal – the dreaded annual review – so they suggested that each member of staff should meet with their boss for an informal one-to-one chat every month.

The informal one-to-ones meant that difficult issues could be identified earlier and tackled more quickly, before they became serious. For example, Julie's boss saw that she was really struggling not only with her own workload but also that of a colleague who was on long-term sick leave, so her boss was able to bring in help more quickly. And Peter had been on a really helpful report-writing course, the results of which his boss asked him to pass on to others at their staff meeting. The introduction of one-to-ones meant that relations between colleagues and managers were better, managers were better informed about their staff and annual appraisals became far less of an ordeal.

Developing your staff

Your appraisals will show the development needs of your staff, and your next task is to work on these. People may have both immediate development needs (such as learning how to use new software or improving their time-management skills) and longer term needs (such as developing their leadership skills). Your goal should be to enable each person to achieve their full potential.

It is hoped that you will have finances set aside in your budget for training.

Training courses

As a manager you should consider the best ways to develop your staff. For example:

- **on-the-job training**: directly relevant to individuals – but you need to find an effective trainer
- **in-house training**: useful if your whole organization needs to develop certain knowledge or skills but may not be relevant to particular individuals
- **external training** led by a professional expert
- **personal coaching/mentoring**: see below.

On-the-job training

Rose was seconded one afternoon a week for several weeks to help Sarah, a new team member, learn how to use the new software. First, Rose demonstrated how to operate an aspect of the software, explaining as she did so. Sarah then had a go herself while Rose talked her through it. Finally, Sarah did the task and explained what she was doing to Rose, who was delighted with the results. Using a step-by-step showing and telling method, Sarah quickly learnt how to use the software.

In looking for courses, consider:

- the outcomes of the course: what will your colleagues be able to do as a result of attending a particular course?
- the background and credentials of the trainers.

After a training course, it is important to have some form of evaluation to ensure that some of the principles 'learnt' on the course have been digested and integrated into your colleague's work practices. Remember: 'use it or lose it' – apply what you have learnt or you will forget it.

Benefits of an outside facilitator

I was due to lead an in-house half-day training session on report-writing skills. I arrived early at the company's offices, as I like to, and was offered a cup of coffee by one of the people who was to attend the course. Another member of staff's immediate response to the offer was, 'Well, you never make me a cup of coffee!' I immediately sensed tension in the organization. The course went very well, and I was commended for having enabled two different groups who normally didn't talk to each other to work together successfully. Sometimes inviting an outside facilitator into a company can achieve significantly more than a colleague within the company.

Coaching and mentoring

Coaching and mentoring are more personal and direct ways of developing a colleague and their skills. The differences could be summed up as follows:

Coaching	Mentoring
More short term	Often more long term
More formal and structured	More informal
Is directed at specific issues or the development of specific skill areas	Considers the person as a whole and provides guidance in career development
Could be undertaken by your line manager or even a colleague on the same level as you but with more experience	Undertaken by an individual higher up in your organization (but not your boss) or from a different organization

A good coach or mentor will:

● be good at listening to what the person being coached is saying and not saying – they will be able to 'read (and hear) between the lines' and ask good questions
● not always respond with answers but will encourage the person being coached to actively come up with solutions to difficulties – they are more likely to take action if they have worked through the issues for themselves than if a coach has simply provided an answer
● bring a different way of thinking about an issue or a problem as they seek to understand it.

Discussing aspirations

Sarah met regularly with Janet, her mentor. Janet wasn't Sarah's line manager, so Sarah felt able to discuss her work freely and confidentially with Janet. In particular, Sarah was able to talk through her aspirations. The mentoring included discussion of Sarah's short- and mid-term training needs and, after the mentoring sessions, Sarah was able to approach her line manager to discuss these with her.

Summary

Today, we've looked at:

- recruiting the right staff
  - defining jobs and people
  - job descriptions and person specifications
  - advertising jobs
  - interviewing staff
- a range of ways to motivate your staff equally so that they feel valued and appreciated
- performance management
  - appraisals (formal)
  - one-to-ones (informal)
- developing your staff
  - training
  - coaching and mentoring.

Next steps

1 Look at your job description and the job descriptions and person specifications of members of your team. In what ways do they need refining to reflect what you all actually do?

2 Think of members of your team who are well motivated. What can you do to motivate them even more?

3 Think of members of your team who are poorly motivated. What can you do to motivate them more?

4 Read any sections of your Employees' Handbook with which you are unfamiliar.

5 Check that the development needs identified in your appraisals link in with your organization's training and development needs.

6 Consider whether you need a personal coach or mentor and, if so, what you will do next.

SUNDAY MONDAY TUESDAY WEDNESDAY THURSDAY FRIDAY SATURDAY

Questions (answers at the back)

1. When drawing up a job description:
   a) rush it through, knowing it will change quickly anyway ❑
   b) spend so much time revising the existing one that you miss the deadline you have set yourself ❑
   c) use the existing one, without checking whether it is still valid ❑
   d) prepare it carefully so that it reflects the job's main purpose and responsibilities. ❑

2. Preparation for an interview is:
   a) a nice-to-have if you have the time ❑
   b) a luxury ❑
   c) essential ❑
   d) unimportant. ❑

3. When motivating staff you should show them:
   a) that you don't care about them ❑
   b) that they are valued ❑
   c) that you are the boss ❑
   d) the door. ❑

4. Appraisals should always be:
   a) only positive ❑
   b) constructive ❑
   c) negative ❑
   d) unfair. ❑

5. In an appraisal it is important to:
   a) let the person being appraised talk ❑
   b) keep the person being appraised silent ❑
   c) not tackle difficult issues ❑
   d) talk only about difficult issues. ❑

6. When setting objectives, they should be SMART. S stands for:
   a) strange ❑
   b) slippery ❑
   c) specific ❑
   d) silly. ❑

7. Regular, informal one-to-ones are a good way of:
   a) replacing yearly appraisals ❑
   b) allowing difficulties to be discussed openly at an early stage, before they become serious ❑
   c) avoiding difficult issues ❑
   d) getting to know your boss. ❑

8. After a training course, evaluation is:
   a) a waste of time ❑
   b) essential ❑
   c) a nice-to-have ❑
   d) a luxury. ❑

9. In a business sense, a coach is:
   a) an experienced person from outside your organization who will guide you informally in the long term ❑
   b) a colleague who will deal with a short-term issue that you have ❑
   c) a long-distance bus ❑
   d) your manager. ❑

10. A good coach or mentor will:
    a) only listen and nod wisely ❑
    b) be no help at all to you ❑
    c) talk and advise you a lot ❑
    d) listen and encourage you to work out answers. ❑

SUNDAY

MONDAY

TUESDAY

WEDNESDAY

THURSDAY

FRIDAY

SATURDAY

TUESDAY

Managing a team

We're used to thinking about sports teams such as football teams, with forwards whose main responsibility is to score goals, midfielders who set up attacks, and defence and the goalkeeper to stop their opponents from scoring.

I once played the clarinet (fairly badly, and I'm not being modest) in a youth band. We gave a series of public concerts. There was nothing like it – my huffing and puffing as a second clarinettist somehow contributed to a gloriously energetic whole ensemble.

So what is a team? It's a group of different people working together towards a common goal. Let's break this definition down into its parts:

- 'A group of different people'. You will have a diverse range of people in your team with different skill sets, personalities and styles of working. This is the team's strength, not a weakness. What would life be like if we were all exactly the same?
- 'Working together towards a common goal'. It is hoped that your team is not just sitting round talking about nothing in particular but is focused on achieving a definite goal or goals.

Today we will look at:

- the diversity of your team members
- developing strong teamwork
- delegating work to your team.

The diversity of team members

The key factor here is that team members bring a valuable and wide range of different roles that complement one another: one person's weakness is balanced out by another person's strengths.

So what are the different roles?

A widely known set of different roles was developed by Dr Meredith Belbin as he looked at how members of teams behaved. He distinguishes nine different team roles:

- **Plant:** creative, good at coming up with fresh ideas and solving difficult problems in unconventional ways.
- **Resource investigator:** outgoing, good at communicating with outside agencies
- **Co-ordinator:** good as chairperson, focusing team members on the goals; a good delegator.
- **Shaper:** dynamic action person who can drive a project forward through difficulties.
- **Monitor/evaluator:** able to stand back and bring objective discernment.
- **Team worker:** bringing harmony and diplomacy for good team spirit.
- **Implementer:** dependable, efficient, practical organizer.
- **Completer/finisher:** able meticulously to follow through on details to complete a project.
- **Specialist:** giving expert technical knowledge.

For further details and information on how to identify colleagues' different roles, see www.belbin.com.

I led an away day for a group I'm connected with. As we began to work together as a team, I ended up (re-)discovering that I had skills in co-ordinating and chairing, so I was formally asked to chair meetings. Of course, some people offer more than one role. For example, our resource instigator, who is good at communicating with many outside contacts, is also an excellent team worker who brings tact and good spirit to team meetings.

This analysis is useful since it can reveal that there may be gaps; your team may be lacking certain skills, which you can

then seek to cover. For example, the discussion above revealed that we had no monitor/evaluator who could stand back and objectively assess ideas. Identifying someone with those skills was therefore one of our aims.

As well as the different roles that people play, team members should be just that: team members, willing to work alongside others. The word 'synergy' has come to the fore in recent years. It is often defined as 2 + 2 = 5, i.e. when two groups of two people work together, the result is greater than the sum of their individual skills. Something extra happens: the combined effect is greater.

Settling into a new role

Andrew had worked in a remote part of the country. He was used to facilitating the development of projects by email and in a few face-to-face meetings. When he later got a job working as a member of a team, he found it difficult to settle into the role. He was not flexible enough and was used to getting his own way, and would tend only to work with others if he was leading a project rather than working on projects led by others. He had to learn to work with others.

SUNDAY MONDAY TUESDAY WEDNESDAY THURSDAY FRIDAY SATURDAY

Developing strong teamwork

As team leader, you are responsible for encouraging your team. What we discuss here builds on motivating your staff, which we considered on **Monday**. Here we are concerned with encouraging members of your team to work together successfully. To do that, you need to:

- Communicate a vision. Where is the team going? What is its purpose? You need to present a strong and inspiring vision of your goals.
- Set your team goals clearly. There is nothing like an abstract statement that is not earthed in reality to turn people off. It is hardly surprising that colleagues come out of a team meeting feeling cynical when a vision has been outlined but no practical implications have been drawn from that vision. A vision must be turned into practical steps.
- Ensure that your values as a team are agreed. Do team members trust and respect one another? Do individuals feel important and part of something bigger than themselves? Encourage team members to remain positive, to believe in the strength and unity of the team.
- Clarify the responsibilities of each member of the team so that each individual knows their own responsibilities and those of the other members of the team. Different members of the team will bring different skills – so play to colleagues' strengths. Don't give the responsibility of chairing a meeting to someone who is unclear or indecisive.
- Ensure that lines of authority and responsibility are clear. Be clear about whether individual team members have authority to spend sums of money up to a certain amount, or whether they should direct all requests for purchases through you, as team leader.
- Be flexible about what is negotiable and try to accommodate different styles of working. Listen to suggestions from colleagues. Be prepared to 'think outside the box' to creatively challenge existing patterns of thinking and working and find solutions to difficulties.

- Be fair and treat all your colleagues equally, even though you may like some more than others.
- Make sure that team members all work as hard as each other and 'pull their weight'. You cannot afford to carry 'passengers' – those team members who work significantly less than others.
- Show enthusiasm in your work. Enthusiasm is infectious, and so is the lack of it. If you are half-hearted it will show in your tone of voice and body language, and colleagues will be aware that you may be saying all the right words but not believing them yourself.
- Encourage openness. As far as you can, involve members of the team in making decisions. Bring out those who are shy and use your skills of diplomacy to quieten those who talk too much.
- Encourage team members to use their initiative. They do not always need to come back to you to solve small difficulties but can be enterprising and resolve issues themselves.

The four stages of team building

A project team was appointed to develop a change-management strategy for a project. When the project team first met, everyone was friendly and there was a sense of excitement as the leader explained the project's aims and they began to get to know one another and work out their roles (known as 'forming'). Fairly quickly, however, issues began to surface as different colleagues had diverging ideas and conflicts began to emerge ('storming'). Fortunately, the team leader stepped in and acted as mediator.

Gradually, team members worked through these challenges and, although discussions still became heated at times, they began to trust one another and were able to reach broad agreement on the way ahead ('norming'). They realized that getting the project completed was more important than protecting their own positions. They

> were then able to work well together to formulate and eventually implement the strategy ('performing').
>
> The names of the four stages were first proposed by American psychologist Bruce Tuckman in 1965.

- Encourage colleagues to look out for one another so that, for example, when one colleague is struggling, a fellow team member can step in and help.
- Challenge the team to work even more effectively. Don't encourage them to sit back but be constantly on the lookout for better ways of doing things that save time or money. For example, are team members entering the same data into two different spreadsheets? Combine them into one, so that the task is not duplicated.
- Set in place effective monitoring controls to track what you are doing (see also **Wednesday**) and then evaluate your progress regularly. For example, if you find that staff expenses claims are not being properly checked, then you must act on this promptly.
- Celebrate success. Recognize the success of individuals. In some cultures colleagues are shy or embarrassed about doing this, but it is an important part of valuing and appreciating people. Celebrate team success. If you have completed a project, go out and mark the occasion by doing something different, such as having a special lunch or an evening meal. Such times help develop a sense of belonging to a team.
- Give feedback. As team leader you should give informal feedback to team members on whether they are doing well ... or not so well. Be specific (e.g. 'I thought the tone of your email in response to the complaint was excellent.'); encourage accountability and deal with difficulties sooner rather than later so they do not become serious.
- Provide opportunities for members of your team to approach you if they need help. You should not be aloof.
- Encourage fun. Hold team-building days where you deliberately mix people up into different groups from those they are normally in. Set tasks in which the groups compete

against one another. The resulting banter will produce laughter and relax people, and you will see sides of people that you have not seen before.

> ## Good team meetings
>
> Nabila was a good team leader. The meetings she led were particularly good. She kept close to the agenda, which had been circulated in advance, and she followed up the action points from the previous meeting. She gave out general information about how the company was performing and led fruitful discussions on how her unit could improve their efficiency even further. She was particularly good at encouraging everyone to participate and express themselves. She always summarized the discussions and came to a clear decision about the next step. She made sure minutes were circulated promptly after meetings so that colleagues were all clear about what they should do. The result was that colleagues in her team all felt inspired and well motivated.

Delegating well

There are lots of reasons why managers don't delegate: you think you can do it better yourself, members of the team are too busy, the task is too urgent, your colleagues aren't quite ready to take on such demanding work. Most of these reasons are essentially about the fact that you don't trust members of your team to carry out the tasks. But when will they be fully ready? When will they have enough time?

You need to adopt three approaches:

- **Plan ahead as much as you can.** Spend time doing this. You know when key tasks (e.g. the annual budget) are required. Build sufficient planning time into your diary (paper, electronic, digital, in the cloud, wherever – but make sure you have some means of planning!).
- **Delegate work to those who are nearly ready to do it.** No one is ever fully ready. Were you? The delegated tasks will stretch those who are nearly ready for them, but that's what you want, isn't it?
- **Delegate more rather than less.** There are a few matters you cannot delegate (e.g. managing the overall team, allocating financial resources, dealing with confidential matters of performance management and promotion), but you can and should delegate many of your actual work tasks and some routine admin activities.

How to delegate

So, you've decided to delegate tasks. How do you go about doing this? Here are some steps:

- Know your team. Who would be the best person to carry out the tasks you want to delegate? Remember the suggestion above: choose colleagues who are nearly ready. If no one is at that level, then provide training so that at least some of them are. Share the load wherever possible. But don't delegate too much work to your best colleague.

- Be clear about the tasks you want to delegate. This is the most important part of delegating. Don't give vague instructions (e.g. 'Could you just write a short report on failings in security?'); be specific. Explain yourself well: 'I'd like a ten-page report giving examples of major security breaches together with possible reasons behind them and recommendations on how to avoid them in future.' Allow plenty of time to explain the task and give your colleague the opportunity to ask questions to clarify what you want them to do.

- Check that the person has understood the task you want them to undertake. Do not just ask, 'Have you understood what I want you to do?' Ask, for example, 'Could you summarize what you will be doing?' Their response will show how much they have understood.

- Give background details, so that the person knows why they are doing the task and where it fits into the overall scheme of things, but without giving an exhaustive account of all the details.

- Where possible, follow up any spoken instructions in writing with a full brief, outlining the work.

- Break down the task into its parts. Write clear briefing instructions, giving concrete examples of what needs to be done.

- State the date and time by which you want your colleagues to complete the work. Remember that what may take you (with all your experience) only half a day will probably take them much longer – perhaps two days.

- Agree how often you want the person to report back to you, particularly (but not only) when they have completed certain agreed targets.

- If a colleague is slow at doing their work, ask them to give you a progress update at the end of each day.

- Be clear about the authority and responsibility you are giving the person. After all, you remain ultimately responsible as manager even though you have delegated the work.

- Supervise their work properly: provide the necessary equipment and other resources they need.
- Let the person decide the details of how they will undertake the work. Allow them to do the work in their own style.
- Where problems or difficulties arise, encourage the person to come to you with them but also to bring their thoughts on possible solutions, together with figures on financial costings for such solutions and the time they would take. This makes better use of your time: they are closer to the details of the task than you are. Your task is then to make a decision based on their suggestions.
- Provide sufficient additional coaching or training to enable the person to undertake and complete the task.
- When they have completed the task, thank the person to whom you delegated the work, expressing your appreciation. Recognize them and their achievement.

A growing confidence

Steve joined a charity as a volunteer some years ago. He showed interest in going further and was given some simple administrative tasks to do, which he completed well. Eventually he started to help in finance and after a few years became a Finance Assistant. With the Finance Director being on leave for a month, the charity had to complete the figures for September within five working days of the month end. Steve took control for the first time and actually calculated the figures in four days, allowing the other directors to sign them off on the fifth day. Steve was a real asset to the charity and he went on to study for a professional accountancy qualification. This all happened because his bosses saw his potential and gave him the opportunity to grow and so his confidence increased.

Summary

Today, we've looked at:

- the diversity of your team members
- appreciating the different roles people play
- filling gaps for missing roles
- developing strong teamwork
- motivating your team to work together as a unit, with each member playing to their strengths
- establishing a strong vision and clear goals
- ensuring each member of the team knows what their responsibilities are
- delegating well
- planning ahead
- giving clear instructions on the task you are delegating, especially on what the end result is (e.g. a report of one or ten pages?) and when you want the work
- trusting colleagues to whom you are delegating work.

SUNDAY

MONDAY

TUESDAY

WEDNESDAY

THURSDAY

FRIDAY

SATURDAY

Next steps

1 Using the Belbin analysis (see also www.belbin.com), consider what role you play.

2 Again using the Belbin analysis, consider what roles are played by others in your team.

3 What practical steps can you as team leader take to develop even stronger teamwork among your team?

4 Does each member of your team understand clearly what their individual responsibilities are? Does each team member know the others' responsibilities?

5 Think about what work you can delegate. Plan ahead.

6 Are you clear when you explain the tasks you need to delegate? Do you trust members of your team to undertake the work you have given them?

Questions (answers at the back)

1. A team is:
a) a group of individuals ❏
b) a group of individuals who work well together ❏
c) a group of individuals who work well together towards a common goal ❏
d) a group of individuals who work badly together. ❏

2. When looking at people's roles, it is important that:
a) everyone has the same role ❏
b) there should be a healthy mix of different roles ❏
c) no one knows their role ❏
d) no one should have more than one role. ❏

3. When encouraging effective teamwork, focus on:
a) the strengths of the team ❏
b) your favourites in the team ❏
c) past failures of the team ❏
d) weaknesses in the team. ❏

4. Effective team members:
a) criticize one another publicly ❏
b) don't care at all about other team members ❏
c) form cliques in the team ❏
d) remain positive, believing in the strength of the team. ❏

5. When giving feedback to a colleague whose work is consistently below standard:
a) avoid discussing it for fear of giving offence ❏
b) discuss it with them sooner rather than later ❏
c) talk about it at a team meeting ❏
d) talk about it every time you see them. ❏

6. When a team member approaches you with an idea:
a) ignore them ❏
b) listen to them and consider it ❏
c) listen to them but forget it immediately ❏
d) think you know better than they do. ❏

7. When delegating work:
a) don't worry about explaining a task as the team member will pick up what is needed ❏
b) explain quickly so you can get on to more important tasks ❏
c) explain the task clearly. ❏
d) Sorry, what is delegating? ❏

8. When delegating work:
a) check occasionally, giving your colleagues the freedom to make mistakes ❏
b) check constantly to make sure they know you're the boss ❏
c) never monitor their work ❏
d) forget you ever gave them work in the first place. ❏

9. When a team member brings a problem to you, encourage them also to bring:
a) a pizza ❏
b) ten different ideas as to how you might solve it ❏
c) a further problem while they are talking to you ❏
d) a thought through solution. ❏

10. When a task has been completed well by a colleague you should:
a) praise them because you like them personally ❏
b) forget all about it ❏
c) recognize their achievement ❏
d) ignore them because you mustn't show favouritism. ❏

WEDNESDAY

Managing your work

Your work as a manager is primarily about managing people and teams. However, to enable you to work efficiently and effectively in those areas, you will also need to learn how to deal with the systems that make up a significant part of your work as a manager.

So today we're concerned with:

- thinking strategically and setting goals
- setting and managing budgets
- developing other systems
- solving problems and making decisions
- dealing with change.

Some of these procedures may seem dry and boring, but learning these skills will provide a firm support for your work. Without them, you would not know where you were, where you were going, nor what the costs were, and you would sink under a weight of problems. With these systems in place you will know your aims and goals and what your costs are, and will be able to work well, solve problems and make good decisions.

Thinking strategically

You need to stop and think about what you want to achieve. Double your profits? Open ten new shops in the next two years? Have a new office on every continent? Whatever your aims, you need to think strategically and focus your thoughts. Here are some questions to help you do this:

● What is your destination? Where are you trying to take your organization? What results (outcomes) do you want to achieve? For example, using the tool of change management (see below), you might want to change your organization and move it on to embrace fresh ideas and manufacture a new range of products.

● What steps (goals) can you set that will be important stages on your journey to that destination? Remember that the goals should be SMART (specific, measurable, agreed, realistic, timed – see **Monday**) so that you know if and when you have achieved them.
● Who else will you involve in this planning process? Your plan should not simply be the result of your own thinking;

it will be the joint effort of your senior managers and other colleagues in your team.

● What assumptions does the plan make? For example, does it assume a certain figure for customer demand for a product that is based on a particular rate of growth in the overall economy? What will happen if that growth figure is not met?

● Have you fully considered the basic resources of time, finance and personnel? How long will your project take? How much will it cost? Do you have the staff to undertake it? If not, where will you find them?

● Have you broken down your plan into manageable parts? Add further details and information on the key issues regarding the basic time, finances and personnel.

● What contingency factors are you building into your budget? Ten per cent is a figure widely quoted to cover unforeseen costs.

● Is the quality of your work and its outputs a priority? Don't accept second best. Make sure you get things right first time.

A SWOT analysis

A SWOT analysis examines your:

● Strengths: what is your company or organization good at? What do you do better than your competitors? What is your unique selling point (USP)?

● Weaknesses: what is your company or organization weak at? What do you have a poor reputation for?

● Opportunities: what directions and trends are there that you could profitably follow up?

● Threats: what problems does your company or organization face at the moment, e.g. increased competition from other companies or constraints on your company's income?

Thinking about these issues will enable you to make good use of the strengths and opportunities and minimize the weaknesses and threats. Undertaking a SWOT analysis is not an end in itself; you need to progress and deal with the issues raised.

Putting goals into action

So you've set out a grand strategic plan and identified certain goals at stages on the way to fulfilling that plan. What are the next steps? You need to clarify the roles of your colleagues. You don't want two people each doing the same work, while neglecting other work that needs to be done.

As we saw on **Tuesday**, an important part of managing teams is to clarify the roles of the different members. Not only should each person know their own role and responsibilities, but also the different roles and responsibilities of the other team members, so that everyone knows what is required of them and where they fit into the overall strategy.

When you give targets and goals to colleagues, they know what to aim at and that is likely to increase their motivation as well as stretching their abilities.

> ## Setting specific goals
>
> As the manager of a café, Teresa was wise – she knew that the goals she set her team members had to be few in number ('less is more'). She also knew that they had to be specific – not simply, 'Be more customer focused' but, 'Take customers' orders for drinks within two minutes of their sitting down at their table.' And by looking at the numbers of customers who came into the café at different times during the day, she recruited sufficient staff for the peak periods to help meet her targets.

Setting and managing budgets

As a manager you will need some financial skills. Some of these may be more technical, others are relatively easy to grasp.

Setting the budget

The basis for a future budget will be the budget for the current year, and you will need several different kinds of accurate information to enable you to make good decisions. Such information will include:

- data so far this financial year
  - income
  - expenditure
  - significant points of variance between actual and budgeted income and expenditure, and reasons for such variances
  - profit or loss and, if the latter, a consideration of the reasons
- aims for next year
- trends for next year that your organization wants to pursue
- increases in pay
- inflation
- improvements in productivity
- plans or projects your organization wants to implement
- contingency.

Putting together a budget for the future is not simply a matter of typing numbers into a spreadsheet. You also need to consider:

- whether the assumptions made are realistic, e.g. will the prices of raw materials remain stable over the next 12 months? Will your company really grow and capture your target of, say, 10 per cent more of the market next year?
- staff costs
- overheads (general business expenses). Do they accurately reflect actual costs?

Managing your budget

One of your responsibilities as a manager may be to manage your team's budget. Again, accurate information is vital. Ensure that your financial software produces regular reports on income and expenditure analysed into 'cost centres', to which particular items of expenditure are allocated. You can then monitor and review income and expenditure and act accordingly.

If you are exceeding your budget, here are some tips to reduce your spending:

- Only spend money on essentials – what you definitely need – not on 'nice-to-have' items. You may be able to postpone buying certain services or products.
- Think of ways in which you can work more effectively and efficiently:
  - Are all your meetings necessary? The agendas at most of the meetings at one company I came across were about the meetings themselves, not about the actual work!
  - Are there some aspects of your work that you could stop doing completely?

- Reduce expenses where possible. Change from first class to standard class travel. Can staff travel at cheaper periods of the day?
- Reduce working hours by stopping overtime or extending the period in which the office is closed for the Christmas and New Year break.
- Freeze posts when colleagues have left. However, this will mean that the remaining members of the team have to take on additional roles and responsibilities, which may not be popular.

	BUDGET 2011/12	Actual	Difference
	£	£	£
PERSONNEL			
Salaries	88,700	89,000	(300)
Expenses	2,500	1,572	928
OFFICE			
Telephone	2,000	1,612	388
Insurance	2,100	2,000	100
Water rates	500	389	111
Heat & light	6,400	7,003	(603)
Photocopier, post & stationery	7,500	9,000	(1,500)
Website maintenance	300	352	(52)
Office furniture/equipment	200	210	(10)
Miscellaneous	500	179	321
MAINTENANCE			
General maintenance	9,000	8,790	210
First aid	1,800	1,840	(40)
Security alarm service	320	600	(280)
Heating service contract	600	750	(150)
Refurbishment	0	0	0
Supplies (kitchen)	1,000	753	247
Miscellaneous	500	310	190
IT EQUIPMENT			
IT Equipment	2,700	2,900	(200)
MISCELLANEOUS			
Conferences	200	0	200
Bank charges	350	358	(8)
Acccountancy fees	1,500	1,652	(152)
CONTINGENCY	12,000		12,000
TOTAL	140,670	129,270	11,400

Comparing budget with actual figures

Notes

- In the 'Difference' column, figures indicate where the actual is less than the budget; figures in brackets show where the actual is more than the budget.
- The figures show that although some expenditure – notably salaries, heat and light, security alarm, IT equipment, heating service contract, accountancy fees and particularly photocopier, post and stationery – were higher than budgeted, because there was a substantial figure for contingency, there was an overall balance of £11,400.

Developing other systems

I remember it well; it was just about the time when we were all getting computers. Every day for a month I reflected on the fact that I was repeating the same tasks every month. I needed systems and procedures – or at least forms to fill in – so I didn't have to 'reinvent the wheel' every month. So I developed some procedures and systems – spent time to save time – so that I could concentrate on the real work, the content of the procedures, rather than on the procedures themselves.

There will be a whole range of procedures that you need to complete regularly, such as:

- filling in/checking time sheets
- checking the photocopier usage
- ensuring that holiday procedures are being followed
- preparing for annual goal setting
- ensuring that your policies on Health and Safety and Data Protection are being complied with
- preparing for the annual budget
- managing your budget.

You need 'operational controls'. You can introduce all sorts of wonderful procedures, but experience shows that they all fall by the wayside if no one is checking up on the processes. Anything you say you are going to do on a regular ongoing basis, or any statements that you make about what senior management needs, must be checked.

Management reporting

You will need to put in place processes, linked with your accounting systems, to provide clear and consistent information to your senior managers on such key issues as cost, quality, outputs and growth. These will be in the form of key performance indicators (KPIs), which give an objective measurement of how well or how badly the strategy of your company or organization is being implemented.

Your goal is to enable senior managers to make informed decisions not only so they can analyse performance against targets but also so they can plan strategically for the future.

Solving problems and making decisions

Much of your time as a manager will be taken up with the two processes of solving problems and making decisions.

Solving problems

Here are some guidelines:

- Ask whether it is your problem. Is it your responsibility to respond to it, or is it someone else's? Or is it just one of those things you have to live with? If the problem is yours:
  - How important is it? Will solving it have a significant effect on your work? Apply the Pareto principle (named after the Italian economist and sociologist, Vilfredo Frederico Pareto (1848–1923) and also known as the 80:20 rule). For example, 80 per cent of problems may come from three major issues and 20 per cent from 20 minor issues. It's better to concentrate on the 80 per cent caused by the few major issues than become preoccupied with the 20 per cent caused by many issues.
  - How urgent is it? If the problem will become more serious if you do nothing about it, then act sooner rather than later. Occasionally, however, some problems can turn into positive opportunities, so don't always think you have to solve them all.

- Get to the root of the problem. Think; discuss with other colleagues; analyse the problem by separating it into its parts to help you define it more closely and understand it more fully.
  - In particular, concentrate on the causes – not the symptoms or effects – of the problem. So if someone's work is below standard, don't keep on moaning about it by giving examples. Instead, try to find out why and ask whether they need training, or consider whether they would be more suitable for different kinds of work.
  - Keep on asking questions, especially the question 'Why?', so you gain a complete understanding of the real issue. Often it's more about asking the right questions than giving the right answers.
- Gather information about the extent of the problem. If the quality of products is falling, does this affect 1 in 1,000 products or 900 in 1,000?
- Concentrate on the big issues. Don't get bogged down in detail. ('He's always late, because the number 101 bus is always late. Here's the times it's turned up over the last month: 8.12, 8.31, ...'.)
- Use your experience. As you progress as a manager, you will develop that sense of 'I've been here before. How did I solve the problem last time?'
- Consider different responses. Here are some techniques you could use to respond creatively to problems:
  - Brainstorm: take a flipchart. Ask one person to state the problem and then get them to write down ideas thinking about the problem from different angles, e.g. your customers' and your competitors'. Encourage participants to build on one another's ideas; don't criticize or evaluate them. At the end, participants agree how to take the best ideas to the next stage.
  - Draw up a flow chart that shows the different stages that led to a problem, how the problem is expressed (i.e. its symptoms) and the connections between the problem's causes and effects.
  - Think 'outside the box'. Is the problem difficult to put into words? Then draw it or work out if you are better explaining it using a painting, a piece of music or by role play.

- Draw a pattern diagram (see **Thursday**).
- Conduct a SWOT analysis (see earlier today).

Making decisions

Here are some guidelines:

- **Act, don't over-analyse.** By temperament, I'm an analyser. Fortunately my wife is an action person – that's why we make a good team. Ultimately, you need to stop analysing and make a decision.
- **Review the possible solutions.** We don't live in a perfect world, so it's unlikely that every decision you make will be a perfect one. You may have to make a decision now, with the full knowledge that you may need to return to the issue in two years' time.
- **Discuss the matter with other colleagues.** If necessary, consult an expert. They may shed light on issues, risks or alternatives that you have not thought of. Try to reach a collective decision: at least if the decision is wrong, blame will come to the whole group and not just one person. If necessary, discuss a delicate issue with a colleague in private rather than in a group, as 'political' matters may come into play in the wider group.

Dealing with change

One key aspect of your role as a manager may be change management: you may need to make significant changes to your operating procedures to reduce costs. What you need to do is move colleagues on from the 'We've always done it this way' way of thinking, which may be firmly embedded in their culture.

Responses to change

- **People don't like change.** 'We've always done it this way' is the mantra they may repeat. 'Things worked as they did – why do we need to change?'

- **People are uncomfortable with change.** Many people like routine, and their patterns of life will be disrupted if changes are brought in.
- **People feel threatened by change.** Change can create fear of the unknown. Changes may affect a colleague's sense of identity.

Leading change

Here are some of the keys to leading change.

Understand your organization

What is the organization's general atmosphere? Is there a climate for change? Is the prevailing mood one of positive confidence, a 'can-do' supportive mentality, or are attitudes negative and cynical with a lot of back-biting and in-fighting? Be aware not only of what is going on at the centre of your organization but also at its edges, and what is not (or no longer) going on. Talk to your colleagues, and even more importantly, listen to them (see also **Thursday**).

Emphasize the vision, the goal

Don't get sidetracked by minor issues. Your organization's mission statement may be concerned with serving the community, but that focus may have got lost. Refocus your team members' vision on that goal so that they understand it. In managing change, you will constantly need to explain why you are doing what you are doing.

Convince colleagues that there must be change

When you are trying to introduce change in an organization, it is vital that this is not seen as only one person's favourite subject. Senior managers must be committed to change and the results of the changes must be shown to have a direct relationship with one of your organization's key goals. It is vital to have a good strategy in place that will move from your vision and goal through your values to help earth your plans in reality. You need to explain clearly to team members why changes are needed (e.g. because of falling productivity or decreasing profits as companies are choosing your competitors) and the benefits changes will bring.

Develop fresh values
Turn your vision and goal into values that determine the emphasis and ethos of your organization. Make them as practical and simple as possible. (I led a writing course for a group of leading police officers and kept on asking them to simplify their values in ordinary words. It took two hours, at the end of which the boss said, 'Martin, you've changed my writing style in two hours!') You may be able to develop the former values of your organization or you may need to rework them totally.

Involve your colleagues
In the early days of change management, involve the colleagues who will be part of the changes. Don't leave them in the dark: involve them in setting the vision and strategy and in making decisions. Get influential colleagues on your side. Enthuse as many people as you can.

Communicate well
As we will see on **Thursday**, good communication is essential in a company or organization, and this is even more essential when you want to move an organization through change. Rumours

about possible changes to people's jobs, roles and location of jobs can all too easily arise, and these can lower morale and lead to poor motivation. Clear, well-thought-out, planned communications are vital in order to bring your colleagues with you. Formal, public communications are significant, but the informal, passing-in-the-corridor type conversations are also important. One long-standing friend of mine deliberately allows extra time on a visit to the farthest end of his organization's workplace so that he can stop and talk to people on the way.

Recognize positive achievements and efforts, celebrate milestones. One club I'm involved with in my spare time celebrated the initial decision to change with a meal for the committee in a restaurant.

Stay focused on the goal but be willing to negotiate on the way to reach it

Keep stating your goal and why changes are necessary, but be flexible on the detail and style of the ways in which colleagues can reach that goal, so they feel fully involved. Try not to be deflected from your main goals by colleagues who want to make small unimportant changes.

Go for quick wins

Find an aspect of change that can be implemented fairly quickly and relatively easily and will produce the results you want, to demonstrate to the wider audience that change is happening and to bring about a positive response.

Introducing changes gradually

Martha was promoted to team leader and had many good ideas about changes she wanted to bring in (e.g. team statistics, rotas, new personal targets). However, her colleagues reacted badly to the speed of changes and her mentor had a quiet word with her ('Go for "Evolution" not "Revolution".'). So Martha slowed down and introduced the changes at a more measured pace. The result was that her colleagues' self-confidence increased as they successfully navigated the changes.

Summary

Today has been concerned with managing your work:

- standing back, thinking strategically and setting goals that can then be translated into action
- setting and managing budgets
- developing other systems
- solving problems and making decisions
- dealing with change.

Next steps

1 Do you know the strategic goals of your company or organization?
2 What assumptions do they make? Do you think they are valid?
3 Is your strategic plan well translated into clear goals and targets?
4 How much do you understand the budget and finances of your company or organization? What steps can you take to increase your understanding?
5 What regular activities do you undertake that you can work on more efficiently?
6 What methods can you use to solve the problems you are facing?
7 How can you be more effective in bringing about change in your company or organization?

SUNDAY
MONDAY
TUESDAY
WEDNESDAY
THURSDAY
FRIDAY
SATURDAY

Questions (answers at the back)

1. When translating your strategic plan into goals, the goals and targets should be:
   a) non-existent ☐
   b) many and clear ☐
   c) few and clear ☐
   d) many and vague. ☐

2. In a SWOT analysis, SWOT stands for:
   a) storms, welcome, offices, trouble ☐
   b) study, wheels, origins, time ☐
   c) steps, wisdom, output, thinking ☐
   d) strengths, weaknesses, opportunities, threats. ☐

3. Putting an amount for contingency in a budget is:
   a) a nice-to-have ☐
   b) a luxury ☐
   c) essential. ☐
   d) What is contingency? ☐

4. KPIs are:
   a) Kentucky pink improvements ☐
   b) key performance indicators ☐
   c) kangaroo performance indicators ☐
   d) key performance isolators. ☐

5. When trying to solve a problem:
   a) keep asking 'Why?' until you get to the root of the problem ☐
   b) be satisfied with superficial causes ☐
   c) look at the symptoms of the problem ☐
   d) look at the effects of the problem. ☐

6. When trying to solve a problem:
   a) save money above all ☐
   b) draw diagrams of the car park ☐
   c) gather all the details together ☐
   d) concentrate on the big issues. ☐

7. At work, you sometimes have to spend time to save time.
   a) This is irrelevant. ☐
   b) I haven't got time to consider this. ☐
   c) True ☐
   d) False ☐

8. When introducing change:
   a) criticize colleagues for their poor performance ☐
   b) constantly state why you are making the changes ☐
   c) be silent once you are making the changes ☐
   d) be silent about why you are making the changes. ☐

9. In leading an organization through change, good communication and leadership are:
   a) essential ☐
   b) unimportant ☐
   c) nice to have ☐
   d) a luxury. ☐

64

10. A quick win is:
a) part of a change that you hope will fail ☐
b) an aspect of change you can quickly implement and will produce good results ☐
c) the winning scorer in a football match ☐
d) a celebration of victory. ☐

THURSDAY

Communicating effectively

'I never knew that was happening.' 'No one told me about that.' 'That's the first I've heard about it.' Do these sound familiar?

Communicating well is a significant part of your role as a manager. Roles and responsibilities cross over each other and you can spend a lot of time sorting out who should be doing what, when it would have been better if all that had been clarified earlier.

So today we stand back and consider different ways in which you should communicate as a manager, through listening, emailing, using the phone, writing reports, giving presentations, negotiating and resolving conflict.

We will also look particularly at meetings – their purpose, preparing for them, chairing them, participating in them and following them up – and ways to improve your reading techniques. All these are core skills that you should try to cultivate to become an even more effective manager.

Listening

Listening may seem a strange place to start, but as is often stated, 'God gave us two ears and one mouth', so before we're tempted to speak it is wise to listen.

● Listening focuses on the other person. Often when someone else is talking, we're focusing on what we are going to say in reply. Don't be tempted to interrupt the other person while they are talking. Stop and really listen to what they are saying. Make eye contact with them. Rephrase what they've said in your own way to help clarify the meaning in your own mind (e.g. 'So what you're really saying is that the whole process needs to be looked at again'), a process called 'reflective listening'.

● It values the person you are listening to as an individual in their own right, so that you understand 'where they're coming from', why they are working or speaking as they are.

● Listening encourages you to ask the right questions. As you focus on the other person (not yourself), you will want to know more. We can distinguish:
  – closed questions. These can be answered by a straight 'Yes' or 'No': 'Was the project late?' 'Yes.' 'Will you be able to give me the figures by 5.00 p.m.?' 'No.'
  – open questions. These get people talking, using 'why', 'how', 'who', 'when', 'where', 'what': 'Why do you think the project is running late?' 'Because we didn't plan for the extra work the customer now wants.' Most of the questions you should ask as a manager should be open questions.

● Listening attentively enables you to perceive your colleague's response to what you are saying by being sensitive to their body language and tone of voice, as well as hearing the words they're saying.

● It allows you to 'listen between the lines', to become aware of any underlying messages – your response could be, for example, 'So I guess what you're saying is that you need someone else to help you complete this task on time'.

- It allows you to distinguish between facts and opinions. You will hear both, and you can discern what is objective information and what are subjective thoughts on this information.
- Listening builds trust between people: you show that you are genuinely interested in them. This forms a basis to help you work well with them.

Susie was angry

Susie was angry. She worked late every evening to complete her tasks on the project but she felt her work was not appreciated or valued. It was only when a new colleague, Jan, started to work alongside her that something happened. Jan was concerned less about herself and her own work (which she did well) and more about her colleague – she cared enough to stop and listen to Susie. Susie was in tears as she poured out her heart to Jan, and at the end of their conversation Susie told Jan, 'Thanks for listening. You're the first person I've been able to talk to about these things.'

The basics of communication

In the seminars I lead on communication, I discuss the basics under the headings A I R:

- **Audience**: we adapt what to communicate according to our audience. So, for example, an email to a colleague at the next desk to us will be written in a different tone from one to the company's Managing Director or an external consultant.
- **Intention**: what exactly are you trying to communicate? What is your message? If you are not clear about it, the readers of your email or report won't be clear either.
- **Response**: what are you expecting your colleague to do as a result of your communication? Have you made clear what you want your colleague to do next? You don't want them to say, 'Yes, I get that, but so what?'

Email

Emails are great. We can communicate with colleagues all round the world instantly. But emails also have their disadvantages. For example, we can receive too many unwanted ones that stop us dealing with the tasks we are supposed to be dealing with.

Here are a few tips:

- Put a clear subject in the subject line; this will help your reader know what the email is about.
- Use 'cc' ('carbon copy', from the days of paper) and 'bcc' ('blind carbon copy') sparingly. Only send copies to those who really need to see the email. To explain 'cc' and 'bcc': if I am emailing Colin and cc Derek and bcc Ed, then Colin will see that I have copied the email to Derek but Colin will not see that I have copied the email to Ed. 'bcc' can also be useful for bulk emails when you don't want individuals to know who else is on your emailing list.
- Unless you are writing to a close colleague, include some form of opening and closing greetings. Your organization's policy and your own personality will guide you about what

is acceptable (e.g. I find 'Hi Martin' difficult to accept from someone I don't know at all).

- In a long email, put the key information at the beginning, so that it will be clear as your reader opens the email. Spend some time laying out your email. Plan in advance what you want to say. Group sentences in paragraphs concerned with one subject. Remember that if your message isn't clear to you, then it certainly won't be clear to your readers!
- Keep your sentences to 15–20 words. On one of the courses I teach on clear writing, a participant's key message was buried in brackets at the end of a 67-word sentence!
- Pay attention to the tone of your email. Could what you say be misinterpreted? 'I look forward to receiving your report soon' could be interpreted as 'Why are you late with it?' Add a suitable, sincere closing greeting.
- Make sure the spelling, grammar and punctuation are correct.
- Use abbreviations that are generally known, not obscure ones.
- Avoid capitals, which indicate shouting.
- Include other contact information at the end of your email, including your job title, phone numbers (landline, mobile) and postal address. Your reader might want to phone you to clarify a point.
- As with all forms of communication, check that what you are saying is accurate before you send it. We've all received emails inviting us to a meeting on Tuesday 14 September, only to discover that 14 September is a Wednesday. The result is that many colleagues spend precious time emailing requests for clarification and then having to respond a second time once they have the exact date. It would have been better if the person who originally sent the message had checked the details first.

Reading emails

Try to discipline yourself to opening and responding to emails at fewer points during the day. During periods that require concentrated work, switch your email off. The time taken to open an email and then think, 'I'll just reply to this now I've opened it', adds up and can have a significant effect on your overall work.

Don't forget the phone

To discuss something complex, communicating by telephone is often better than email. Before you make the call, jot down the points you want to discuss.

The phone also remains a useful tool to build and develop professional relationships, since you can react immediately and check whether someone has understood what you are trying to communicate and, if not, you can explain it again differently.

Meetings

Sometimes it seems as if life consists of going from one meeting to another without actually achieving anything. How can we make sure the meetings we attend count? We can consider:

- the purpose of meetings
- preparing for meetings
- chairing meetings
- participating in meetings
- following up from meetings.

The purpose of meetings

Meetings are useful to:

- inform colleagues, e.g. to introduce new goals or give an update on progress
- discuss with colleagues, e.g. plan together the way ahead or evaluate a solution to a problem
- reach a decision and agree the next steps to be taken.

Team meetings are also particularly useful in order to develop a sense of team identity as members interact with one another. As team leader you can use team meetings to motivate your team (look back at **Monday** and **Tuesday**).

Preparing for meetings

The key to a successful meeting lies in the preparation. It is essential that you:

- **Know the purpose of the meeting.** Many of our meetings have no clear purpose and could easily be shortened or even cancelled. You need to be crystal clear about what you are trying to achieve.
- **Plan a venue and time (start, finish) in advance.** I've been to some meetings at the stated venue but arrived there to find the meeting is in a different place
- **Invite the key people to participate in advance.** If you want a boss with a busy diary to be present, then it is no good inviting them the day before; you need to have invited them well in advance. It is also useful if you can discuss in advance, in private with key people, any agenda items that could be controversial.
- **Circulate an agenda in advance.** This means you will have thought about the structure and purpose of the meeting beforehand. Also, circulate important papers with the agenda rather than at the meeting itself. Ideally, such papers should be no more than one page each.
- **Prepare the meeting room.** Plan the seating: chairs around a table invite discussion; a chairperson at the end of a long table with ten seats either side, less so. If a PowerPoint presentation is being given, ensure that a projector and connecting lead are set up. Check that the heating or air conditioning works.
- **Read reports in advance.** If reports have been circulated before a meeting, then read them. I have been in too many meetings where we have sat during the meeting reading material which should have been read in advance.
- **Ensure that you come up with accurate information.** For example, if the meeting is one to monitor progress, take all your latest data on progress with you.

Chairing meetings

The chairperson is the person who sets the tone for the meeting and guides the participants through the discussion. Their tasks include:

- keeping to the agenda so the meeting starts and finishes on time

- introducing and welcoming newcomers, or asking participants to introduce themselves
- reviewing progress on action points from previous meetings
- bringing in key individuals to contribute at appropriate points
- stating key aims and objectives
- summarizing progress of the points being discussed
- drawing together the points discussed, to reach conclusions, to make decisions; if a point has been controversial, the chairperson can express exactly what is to be minuted, to avoid possible misinterpretation later
- ensuring action points are clear, particularly who is responsible for following up particular points. The action points should be SMART (specific, measurable, agreed, realistic, timed – see **Monday**).

A good chairperson is a diplomatic and organized leader, someone people trust and who values, motivates and involves others. Ideally, they will be able to quieten down those who talk too much and draw out those who talk too little but who can still make valuable contributions. A good chairperson will also sense when the time is right to bring a discussion to an end and will be able to come to clear decisions.

Participating in meetings

Everyone has a part to play in a successful meeting. I have never understood how people can come out of a meeting asking, 'What was the point of that?' when they themselves have not contributed anything. Each of us has a role to play by:

- listening well and concentrating: switch off your phone, avoid sending text messages, don't interrupt when someone else is talking
- asking for clarification if we are unsure about a point that has been made: it is highly likely that other colleagues will also want clarification but have been afraid to ask, e.g. for fear of looking ignorant
- being constructive: even if we disagree with what has been said, there are positive ways of expressing a difference of opinion by challenging an idea without angrily criticizing a person expressing an idea or publicly blaming an individual for a wrong action
- confronting issues: focus on the real issues – don't get sidetracked; too many of our meetings avoid discussing 'the elephant in the room', the subject everyone is aware of but is not discussed because it is too uncomfortable
- being willing to change your mind: if you are listening and persuasive arguments have been offered, then allow yourself to be convinced by them and change your opinion about an issue.

Videoconferencing

Videoconferencing means that you can link up with colleagues via the internet and avoid spending time and money travelling. Here are some tips to help you plan a videoconference session:

- Make sure the room in which the meeting takes place has good acoustics and is tidy.
- Agree and circulate the agenda in advance to all participants. Appoint a chairperson who can introduce the participants. Email any special presentations (e.g. PowerPoint) in advance.
- Identify individuals by having cards in front of them with their name on.
- Remind participants to look at the camera while they are talking. Ask participants to listen while other people are speaking.

Follow-up to meetings

A meeting where decisions are made but no one acts on these decisions is a waste of time. If colleagues have action points to pursue, they should follow them up.

The minutes of a meeting are a record of what happened in the meeting, including its action points. The person taking the minutes does not need to write down everything that goes on, but significant decisions, especially the action points concerning dates, schedules and financial matters must be noted specifically.

The sooner the minutes of a meeting are circulated to those who were present and other key colleagues, the more likely it is that people will follow up the action points asked of them.

A good chairperson will also follow through on progress of the key action items; they will not leave it to the next meeting only to discover that action has not been taken and valuable time has been lost.

Writing reports

- As with any other form of communication, think about what you want to say. One good way of helping you to start thinking about a report is to draw a pattern diagram (also known as a Mind Map). Take a blank piece of A4 paper. Arrange it in landscape position and write the subject matter of the report in the middle. (Write a word or a few words, but not a whole sentence.) You may find it helpful to work in pencil, so you can rub out what you write if necessary.
- Now write around your central word(s) the different key aspects that come to your mind. You do not need to list ideas in order of importance; simply write them down. To begin with, you do not need to join up the ideas with lines.
- If you get stuck at any point, ask yourself the question words 'why', 'how', 'what', 'who', 'when', 'where' and 'how much'. These may set you thinking.
- When I do this, I am often amazed at: (1) how easy the task is; it doesn't feel like work! The ideas and concepts seem to flow naturally and spontaneously. (2) How valuable that piece

of paper is. I have captured all (or at least some or many) of the key points. I don't want to lose that piece of paper!

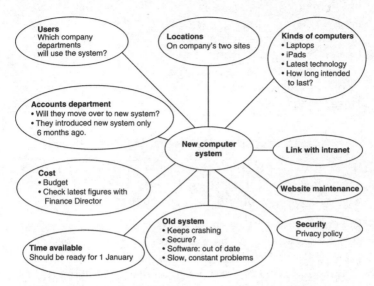

An example of a pattern diagram for a report on buying new computer systems

- Be clear about your audience, intention and response (see earlier today). This will determine, for example, how much information you should include in your reports. If in doubt, discuss with colleagues. In other words, don't agonize over writing ten pages when senior management only want one page.
- Use a report template that your company or organization has already established to give a structure to your report.
- Make sure your message is well planned and well structured.
- Write clearly and, if possible, simply, using only those abbreviations and technical expressions with which the readers of your report are familiar.
- Draft as much as you can to give yourself a psychological boost that you have actually written something. Then go back over your material, editing it.

- Be as concise as possible. You may have heard of the quotation, 'I have written you a long letter because I didn't have time to write you a short one.' Writing concisely is an art to be learnt – but it is very useful. If the report is long, present a one-page summary at the beginning.
- Use correct grammar and proper punctuation. Shortage of time is no excuse for using careless or sloppy English or the forms or abbreviations (textspeak, SMS language) you use to close friends.

Reading more effectively

So far today, we've thought about listening and writing. There are two other forms of communication: reading and speaking. Here are some guidelines to help you read more effectively:

- Decide on your aims in reading a particular text. Do you want simply to check a fact, gain an overall sense of a text, or grasp a detailed knowledge of a subject?
- If you want to undertake a more detailed read of the text:
  - Look out for the signposts: the introduction and conclusions; the words 'firstly', 'secondly'; the beginning of paragraphs; such expressions as 'on the one hand' and 'on the other hand' which guide you through the structure of the text, which can be helpful to your understanding.
  - Reword the main points in your mind, on computer or on paper. Express the author's key points in your own way.
  - Think about the author's argument: do you agree with them? Does the text make assumptions that you disagree with? Ask questions of the text and see if they are answered. Engage your mind.
  - At the end, see if you can recall the main points, or even better, see if you can explain the main points to someone else.

Reading statistics

Here are some guidelines on reading and understanding numbers presented in tables:

- Check the basics: the dates covered; the sources used; the scale used; the context of the figures, e.g. if the figures represent a sample, how large is that sample? Are the assumptions reasonable? Are certain figures omitted? Why? Check the definitions of terms used. Are they sound? If percentages are shown, percentages of what?
- Take one row or column and think through its content and implications to understand the data.
- Compare figures in columns and consider any trends. Do the numbers show a consistent pattern that increases or decreases? For example, is actual expenditure consistently higher than budgeted?
- Consider averages. Calculate the average for a particular row or column and see what variations and exceptions there are. Try to work out reasons for such differences, e.g. variations because of higher or lower income or differing levels of employment.
- Read the text that accompanies the data and check you agree with it; be particularly wary of phrases such as 'significant', 'these figures of course show'.
- Be careful about putting too much confidence in extrapolations of data that assume a trend will continue.

Giving presentations

As a manager, you will be called on at times to give a presentation. Here are some guidelines:

- Prepare by planning well. Know your audience. Senior managers? Colleagues?
- Work out your key messages. Be crystal clear on what you are trying to say. Express it in a maximum of 15 words on paper. Keep your 'headlines' simple. Don't try to cram too much in – 'less is more'.
  - Break down your key points into subpoints. Work on your words. Use short, everyday words rather than longer ones. So, use 'try' rather than 'endeavour'; 'need', not 'necessitate'; 'stop' or 'end' rather than 'terminate'; 'harmful' rather than 'detrimental'.

- Vary the way in which you communicate. Ask questions. Give a case study to back up the point you are making. Be creative. Find a picture that will illustrate your talk (but beware of any copyright issues).
- Work on the different parts of your presentation. Work especially hard on the beginning, so as to capture your audience's attention with your introduction ('Did you know ...?' 'I was reading in today's newspaper ...'), and the end ('So the next step is ...') to draw together and reinforce application of your key points.
- Structure your main points in a logical sequence. If you can structure them by making them all start with the same letter of the alphabet, or with 'ABC' (e.g. one of the talks I give on writing encourages the audience to be accurate, brief, concise), then your points will be more memorable.

● Think what the response of your audience is likely to be. Interested? Bored? In need of persuasion? Sceptical? Anticipate likely reactions by dealing with them in your preparation or in preparing answers to their questions.

● Know how long you will speak for. Fifteen minutes? An hour? People will be grateful if you finish early (but not too early!) but will not appreciate it if you go on too long.

● Prepare any handouts of your presentation. How many will you need? When will you give them out – before or after your presentation?

● Think of the practicalities. What is the layout of the seating? At one workshop I led with 45 delegates I complained that the suggested seating looked too much like that of an exam room, so we adjusted it. Don't forget the heating, lighting and air conditioning.

● Write down your presentation. Either write down (1) every word you plan to say or (2) notes that you can follow. If you do (1), then don't read it out word for word from your paper. Hopefully, your thoughts will have become part of your way of thinking. As you gain more experience, you will probably find you can work from notes.

● Be enthusiastic; be positive. You've a message to declare. Go for it! Be natural; be yourself. It took me years to discover and work out my own style for giving presentations. I was amazed when a colleague contacted me after a space of five years to ask me to lead a workshop at his company. He said, 'I remember your style'.

● Factor in a break. If your presentation is going to last longer than 45 minutes, then schedule a break so that your audience can relax for a few minutes.

If you are using a PowerPoint presentation:

● Allow plenty of time to prepare the presentation, particularly if you are not familiar with the presentation software.
● Don't try to put too much information on the slides. Keep to your headings, not the complete outline of your talk.
● Keep to one main font. Use a large font, ideally at least 28 pt. Aim to have no more than six lines per slide (do you remember peering over people's heads trying to read tiny print on a slide?). A sans serif font is easier to read than a serif one. Headings arranged left (not centred) are easier to read; capitals and lower case letters are also easier to read than text in all capitals.
● Work out which colours work well, e.g. red on grey, yellow on blue.
● Use tables and charts to support your message. Bar charts, pie charts, flow charts giving the key information all work well.

- Use illustrations that support your message, not ones that show off your (lack of!) design or animation skills.
- Don't put the key information at the bottom of slides; colleagues far away from the screen may not be able to see over other people's heads.
- Rehearse the presentation with your notes/text in advance.
- Check whether you or a colleague will supply the projector and leads to connect the projector to your laptop and a screen. Arrive early to set everything up.
- Put your presentation on a memory stick (saved in earlier versions of PowerPoint for good measure) in case your laptop fails and you have to view it from someone else's laptop.
- Make sure that when you give your presentation, your eye contact is with your audience, not with your laptop or the screen.

Negotiating: win-win situations

In negotiating, we are aiming for a win-win situation. (This is different from normal behaviour where one person wins at the expense of another's loss.) For example, my son Ben has just moved to Asia and he wanted to sell his camera. His friend Rob wanted a camera to take photographs on his travels. Ben sold Rob his camera. Both won: both gained what they wanted – Ben money, Rob a camera.

In his book *The 7 Habits of Highly Effective People*, Stephen Covey points out that the key to a win-win situation is our character.

If you're high on courage and low on consideration, how will you think? Win-Lose. You'll be strong and ego-bound. You'll have the courage of your convictions, but you won't be very considerate of others. ...

If you're high on consideration and low on courage, you'll think Lose-Win. You'll be so considerate of others' feelings that you won't have the courage to express your own. ...

High courage and consideration are both essential to Win-Win. It's the balance of the two that is the mark of real maturity. If you have it, you can listen and you can empathically understand, but you can also courageously confront.

The 7 Habits of Highly Effective People Personal Handbook,
Stephen Covey (Simon & Schuster, 2003), p. 91.

Colleagues who negotiate win-wins:

- communicate clearly, honestly and positively
- treat the opinions of others with respect, listening well
- respond constructively to possible areas of improvement.

Based on *The 7 Habits of Highly Effective People Personal Handbook*,
Stephen Covey (Simon & Schuster, 2003), p. 93–4.

A good negotiator

Danielle was respected as a good negotiator in contracts. The secret of her success lay in good planning. She spent a long time thinking through different business models and pricing levels so that when it came to the negotiations, she knew exactly what approach to take. After both sides had presented their initial case, she was sometimes able to detect the weak points in the arguments of the other side and exploit them according to her own personality. When they came to the final bargaining she had clarified the critical issue (the price) in her mind and knew the less significant matters she could be flexible on – she didn't mind bringing delivery of the products earlier by six weeks. She was assertive and firm on what was non-negotiable, however: the price. So she was able to settle and close deals well and arrange the next steps in business relationships between the two sides.

Resolving conflict

At times you are bound to meet conflict. Trust breaks down. Personalities clash. Departments each want a bigger slice of the budget or want to avoid the most cutbacks.

Deal with conflict quickly; tackle the issues. Don't be cautious and fearful about speaking directly and clearly about difficulties.

I've found the books *Difficult conversations: how to discuss what matters most* (by Douglas Stone, Bruce Patton, Sheila Heen), Michael Joseph, 1999, and *The Peacemaker: a biblical guide to resolving personal conflict* (by Ken Sande), Baker, 1991, very useful. The following is based on what those authors helpfully suggest:

- Distinguish the incident – what is happening/happened – from feelings about the incident. Consider separately:
  - The incident – someone said something; someone is to blame. Try to focus on the real issue. Listen closely. Ask open questions. Understand other people's interests as well as your own.
  - Feelings about the incident, e.g. anger, hurt.
  - The identity of the person. Sometimes, a person's identity, including their self-worth, will feel threatened. Calmly affirm your respect for them.
- Do what you can to resolve the issue and maintain the relationship if possible; prepare and evaluate possible solutions to agree on the way forward.

Under pressure

Elaine was under pressure. She was actually doing two jobs, each taking up three days a week. She was getting very stressed and knew she could not continue doing such work indefinitely. At both informal one-to-ones and the formal half-yearly appraisal she expressed frustration with her manager Ron. Ron said he would act to resolve the difficulty, but unfortunately, over a period of several months, nothing happened. He awkwardly avoided eye contact with her whenever they passed in the corridor.

Things turned out better, however, when Ron moved on and was replaced by Sheila. Her motto was 'under-promise and over-deliver' so, for example, when she said she would check the financial data for the previous month by the end of week 3 in the following month, invariably she had completed it by the end of week 2. So within a few weeks of Sheila taking on Ron's role, she had sorted out Elaine's work patterns to everyone's satisfaction. Soon Elaine began to enjoy her work again.

Summary

Today has been concerned with communicating effectively:

- listening well
- asking the right kinds of questions
- communicating in different ways, e.g. email, phone, writing
- running better meetings
- writing better reports
- reading more effectively
- giving good presentations
- negotiating well and resolving conflict.

Next steps

What practical steps do you need to take to improve the following? Choose three areas you particularly need to focus on:

1 your listening skills
2 your questioning skills
3 your planning of emails
4 your writing skills
5 your reading skills
6 your planning of meetings
7 the effectiveness of your meetings
8 your presentation skills
9 your negotiation skills
10 your ability to resolve conflict

Questions (answers at the back)

1. Reflective listening is:
a) thinking about listening ☐
b) rephrasing what someone has said to you ☐
c) listening to yourself while looking in a mirror ☐
d) meditating on life. ☐

2. When sending emails:
a) cc everyone who could be interested ☐
b) use cc sparingly, only to those who really need to see the email ☐
c) keep cc on all the time ☐
d) I don't know what cc stands for. ☐

3. When reading emails:
a) answer them all immediately ☐
b) delay answering them until Friday afternoon ☐
c) look at them at particular times, so you can concentrate on your work ☐
d) never answer them at all. ☐

4. When attending a meeting:
a) arrive late ☐
b) fiddle with a pen ☐
c) arrive promptly, having read the agenda and reports ☐
d) arrive promptly, not having read the agenda and reports. ☐

5. During meetings:
a) be indecisive ☐
b) never reach a decision ☐
c) come to decisions but don't record them ☐
d) come to decisions and ensure they are properly recorded and reviewed. ☐

6. At the end of a meeting:
a) stay behind to clear up ☐
b) forget the action points ☐
c) act on the points that it was agreed you would follow up ☐
d) complain that it was a waste of time. ☐

7. When writing reports:
a) show off everything you have learnt ☐
b) be selective about what you have learnt ☐
c) use long words to try to impress your boss ☐
d) don't worry about wrong grammar, spelling or punctuation. ☐

8. When preparing a presentation:
a) put a maximum of six lines on one slide ☐
b) put all your points and subpoints on one slide ☐
c) put all of your talk on the various slides ☐
d) try to impress colleagues with your animation skills. ☐

9. In resolving conflict:
a) ignore people's feelings ☐
b) don't listen to what happened ☐
c) only listen to people's feelings and ignore the real issues ☐
d) distinguish the real issue from colleagues' emotional responses to the issue. ☐

10. Preparing for negotiations is:
a) a waste of time ☐
b) essential ☐
c) a luxury ☐
d) sometimes worthwhile. ☐

FRIDAY

Managing a project

As part of your work as a manager, you've been asked to manage a project. You feel excited but also rather overwhelmed at the prospect. The challenge seems great. Where do you begin?

- Lay firm foundations as you clarify your project and plan carefully.
- Gather together the key personnel involved in the project and clearly communicate to them the project's aims, outputs and schedule.
- Break down the project into smaller parts.
- Cost your project well as you draw up a budget. Make sure you have rigorous controls in place to monitor costs and quality as you implement the project.
- Implement your project successfully. After preparing well, you can now put the project into practice.
- Complete the project's final stages and evaluate your project. What lessons can you learn for next time? What went well ... and what did not go so well?

Planning your project

When I begin a project, I use a pattern diagram (see **Thursday**) to help me in my initial thinking. If you do the same, all sorts of thoughts will come to you.

For a start, discuss with your end users their precise requirements. What do they want – and what do they not want? Consider the project's context. What needs is it intended to satisfy? How has the present situation developed? How does the project align with the overall strategy of your company or organization?

You can then:

- Work out the best way to deliver the required outputs. What precisely does the customer want to be delivered?
- Consider the size of the team of people you will need in order to meet those requirements.
- Prepare a schedule for the project. When are the final outputs needed? For example, if the project is to complete the manufacture of toys for Christmas, they need to be available for delivery in, say, September not December. Work backwards, including the key stages as you now see them, to where you are now.
- Work out costs and prepare a budget. Make a business case and gain approval for the project from senior management.
- Ensure you have the agreement of senior management for your aims, outcomes and the resources needed. This may involve carrying out a feasibility study to make sure the project is sound.
- Develop monitoring procedures to help you control the agreed costs.
- Assess possible risks you may face. For example: is the authority of the project leader clear? Is the schedule realistic? Have sufficient financial resources been made available?

Assemble a project team

At an early stage in your planning, gather colleagues into a project team to ensure that the preparation is undertaken well. The people or organizations with a strong interest in the outcome of a project are called its stakeholders. Circulate a list of stakeholders, showing their names, job titles, contact details (phone, mobile, email, fax).

The stakeholders would typically be:

- **Project sponsor:** a senior member of staff, e.g. a director, who can prove that the project's costs and benefits are worthwhile. They will also need to convince other colleagues that the project is important enough to pursue given certain resources. They will have the authority to reach decisions and approve the spending of the required money and other resources.
- **Project manager** (probably you): the person who reports to the project sponsor and is responsible for implementing the project. The project sponsor should give the project manager the responsibility and authority to carry out the project.
- **Team members**: the project manager, in liaison with the project sponsor, can delegate tasks to members of the team. If team members are less experienced, then as project manager you will need to train, monitor and supervise your colleagues more.
- **The users** (or customers): the people who will use the end result of the project. It is important not merely to consult such people but to understand their needs and involve them

at every stage of the project so that they 'own' it and feel a valued part of the decision-making process.

● **The suppliers**: the people who carry out tasks or provide services to assist in the completion of the project. They may be within or outside your organization. Examples are colleagues working in departments dealing with sales, accounts or computers. Suppliers will ensure that the requirements of the project are met within the agreed timescale and financial resources.

Updating a website

Jones & Co wanted to update their website to make it more usable by its customers and to enable customers to order goods online. As manager, Sally called together colleagues from sales, IT and marketing departments to discuss how to tackle the project. Because Sally involved colleagues from the different departments, she made sure the project was planned well. At the meeting, they discussed a range of ideas, divided the work into three different stages and allocated someone responsible for each stage, with definite dates given for the completion of each stage. After the meeting, Sally circulated the minutes to each participant. The result was a well-planned basis for the project.

Defining a scope of work

Having undertaken your initial planning, you can now add further detail to the thinking to produce a 'scope of work', a statement of the project's objectives and outcomes. This builds on the information that you have already obtained.

A statement of the scope of work is important for two reasons:

● It may form part of the legal contract between you and outside suppliers. If disagreements arise, the different sides will turn to the contract (scope of work) to read what is stated there about the disputed matter.

● It also provides a definite standard against which progress can be measured.

The scope of work will include statements of:

- the project's objectives, background, scope and limits (i.e. what the project is and is not going to do)
- the customers' expectations – this should specify in detail what the project will deliver (e.g. the exact type and number of products)
- the budget, showing the financial resources needed
- a list of other physical resources (e.g. new offices, computers)
- criteria for acceptance (e.g. if I am writing a book, the publisher will make a payment to me only when they consider the work I deliver is of an acceptable standard)
- a list of the main colleagues on the project team
- delivery dates for the products
- assumptions made about the project; risks that could have an effect on the implementation of the project.

A contract will include a scope of work and will specify payments and payment dates (e.g. linked to the delivery of certain products) and other relevant facts, such as patents on products and rights of ownership.

Dividing up the work

Chris felt overwhelmed by the sheer enormity of the project to begin with, but it seemed less daunting when he broke up the work into separate manageable parts. He did this in a work breakdown structure, which showed the project's various tasks. Although his aim was to list all the significant tasks, he knew he would not achieve that immediately, so he discussed the tasks with more experienced colleagues, developing successively more exact definitions of what he wanted to achieve, until he gradually reached the goal of a full specification. He also compiled a spreadsheet showing the tasks, roles and times needed for the different tasks. He had been advised by his senior manager to make allowances in the schedule for project start-up, administration and holidays and also for staff illness and other possible contingencies that could affect the schedule. He was then in a position to allocate members of his team to the various activities, considering how long each activity would take.

Costing your project
Work out the cost of your project

From the work breakdown structure, you can now begin to assign costs.

- Decide who will undertake the work: you, colleagues in your department, colleagues in other departments, or will you outsource some of the work to an outside supplier? For each one of these, you need to know the hourly (or day) rate of the people concerned. Also check to what extent company overheads are included if your project is charged for colleagues from another department in your organization.
- Decide how much work to outsource to outside suppliers, for example if they have greater expertise than your own staff. You will need to give them a precise brief as to the work required, including schedule, work required and payment. Remember to build into your budget time to brief a range of possible suppliers, evaluate their bids and reach a decision on who to choose, brief the supplier at the outset of the work, administer and keep track of their work.
- Decide an approximate level of contingency to handle risks and other uncertain events that will arise.

Working out your hourly rate

Suppose you earn £20,000 per year. If we divide this figure by the number of days you work productively, i.e. omitting holidays and allowing for illness, this could give 46 weeks per year: £20,000 ÷ 46 = £434.78 per week or £86.96 per day, assuming 5 days per week. If we divide that figure by the time per day you spend working productively, say two-thirds of seven hours (= 4.66 hours), that comes to £18.66 per hour. This is the amount you are paid per hour gross, i.e. before tax and other deductions.

That is only half the story, however. Your actual cost to your organization is about twice that figure, allowing for the overheads, taxes it pays as an employer, rent of office building, heating, power, water, etc. So the cost to your company or organization is £18.66 × 2 = £37.32 per hour.

This means that if a business meeting lasts seven hours and is attended by six colleagues, then the cost of that meeting to the organization is 7 × 6 × £37.32 = £1567.44. This is probably significantly more than you thought!

Return on investment

Return on investment is the percentage return you make over a certain time as a result of undertaking the project. It is calculated according to the formula:

ROI = (profits [or benefits] ÷ investment [your costs]) × 100

One way of considering return on investment is to work out the payback period, the time taken for the profits or benefits to cover the cost of your investment.

For example, a project to train all your staff in report-writing skills might cost £50,000, including fee for tutor, materials and administration. Its benefits could be measured in terms of savings of work time and productivity increases of £60,000 over one year, so the return on investment is (60,000 ÷ 50,000) × 100 = 120%.

Finalize the project budget

Ensure that you have included the cost of:

● colleagues: the time spent by your colleagues, colleagues in other departments, people in outside companies or organizations, including start-up and administration time
● equipment or facilities needed for the project, such as computers or offices
● other human-resource costs such as recruitment and training
● other departments' costs such as IT and marketing.

Your budget should also include:

● cash-flow predictions during the whole of your project
● any income forecasts that are part of the project
● the cost centres to which particular items of expenditure will be allocated during the implementation of the project
● contingency: a figure of about 10 per cent of your total costs is often suggested.

Example of extract of a budget for a conference	
Costs	£
Speaker	4,000
Venue	6,000
Marketing	3,000
Administration	3,000
Office	2,000
Contingency	2,000
	20,000
Income	
Delegates' fees	22,000
Net profit	2,000

You can work out the break-even point (the point at which the money you receive covers your costs). For example, if delegates' fees are £400 each, you will need 50 delegates (50 × £400 = £20,000) to cover costs. So the break-even point is £20,000. If you have more than 50 delegates (e.g. in the example shown the income is £22,000, i.e. 55 delegates at £400 each), a profit is made. If you have fewer than 50 delegates, you will make a loss.

Implementing your project

As you put the project into practice:

- Confirm commitments of the key personnel involved and the financial resources available. Check that they can all start on a certain date or as soon as possible afterwards.
- Continue communicating with the other stakeholders to keep them in the picture about the status of the project.
- Make sure you have defined the activities each person needs to undertake. Look at your work breakdown structure and make sure that it specifies:
  - the work to be undertaken
  - the start and end dates
  - key milestones: when certain proportions of the work are completed; when a certain level of income has been achieved; or when a certain output has been delivered and accepted by the customer/user.
- Keep your work breakdown structure as accurate and up to date as possible.
- Control the project's costs by ensuring you have mechanisms in place to record actual expenditure, assigning costs to particular cost centres.
- Prepare monthly summary statements of actual costs and income against those in the project budget, keeping the budget and cash flow as accurate as possible.
- Plan for change, whether on a significant scale in a major disaster (e.g. an act of terrorism or a prolonged period of severe adverse weather), internal project changes or small changes.
- Keep going, remaining focused, positive and determined.

Rescuing a failing project

Imran was called in to trouble-shoot a failing project. The existing project manager was not coping with the responsibilities of the project. Fortunately, Imran had a good working relationship with him. Imran quickly noticed that basic points were missing: meetings were poorly structured with the barest agenda. During the meetings, discussions rambled on without decisions being made. Even when key action points were agreed, they were not noted, followed through or even reviewed at the next meeting. It was hardly surprising that the project was in a mess! As Imran had good relationships with all his colleagues, he was quickly able to put in place well-structured meetings, good chairmanship, minute-taking, action points and reviews at the next meeting.

He also paid particular attention to making sure there were regular progress reports, showing: a summary of the project's progress; the stages completed in the previous month; the actual hours spent on the various stages; actual costs incurred; variations from expected figures in costs and output, together with reasons for those variations; and finally a forecast of the new final completion date and costs.

With good people-management abilities and detailed task-orientated skills, Imran got the project back on track successfully.

Completing a project

You will have agreed a list of the items you need to complete as clearly defined signs that the project has come to an end. These could include:

- ensuring the output of a certain number of products
- ensuring that the quality of what you deliver reaches the agreed criteria, e.g. verifying that a computer software system fulfils the required specifications

- testing new equipment to make sure it functions to the required standard
- training end users, e.g. by preparing manuals or running courses for those who will use the computer equipment you have installed
- completing final administrative tasks, e.g. final progress reports, especially those concerned with financial resources.

Evaluating your project

The project is complete! You're celebrating and are enjoying the feeling of a job well done. Is there more to be done? Yes: you need to conduct a post-project evaluation. This brings together the project's key points so you can see what went well, what did not go so well and also, significantly, what lessons you can learn for the future.

Acknowledge failures

The critical aspect here is to learn from your mistakes – neither to ignore them and pretend they did not happen nor make them so widely known that blame is attached to an individual for the rest of their working life. If your organization has good relationships, then trust and respect will have developed.

Don't be content with the superficial lesson. Look for the deeper reasons, such as why a project was delayed:

- Were adequate monitoring controls in place?
- Were communications good between colleagues, or were key colleagues not informed about significant decisions?

However, ensure that the evaluation is professional: your purpose is not to attach blame on individuals but to be positive and to outline a few realistic lessons that can be learnt and applied in future projects. For example, don't say: 'Chris forgot to order the spare parts on time', but: 'Checks need to be made in advance that orders for spare parts are submitted two weeks before they are needed.' Any constructive criticism of individuals' contributions should be undertaken privately, not in a wider forum.

A project well delivered

I was recently in charge of a project to deliver 5,000 books to an exhibition in the UK in March. We delivered the text to the printers on schedule in October, but were delayed by packaging difficulties which meant that, with shipping time, the books would not reach the UK until April. We therefore had to send the books by airfreight to meet the March deadline. The result was a satisfied customer: we delivered what we said we would. We focused on fulfilling the customer's expectations, even though we incurred higher costs of airfreight.

We later held an evaluation meeting for this project, at which all the key personnel were present. The decision to send 5,000 copies by airfreight was commended – the books were well received and sold out at the exhibition. Minor suggestions were made to improve the design. Costs were reviewed, which were slightly over budget.

The response to the initial set of books was so good that we agreed to produce a further set for next year. Schedule and costs were agreed. Finally, a suggestion was made to tighten up on our internal communications between team members to make them even more effective. Minutes of the meeting have been circulated to record the lessons learnt.

Recognize success

As well as acknowledging failures, mistakes and where you could have undertaken the work better, also recognize those areas that have gone well.

Identify what you have delivered. For example:

● the desired output in terms of the products, services, etc. delivered
● outputs measured according to the agreed quality standards
● actual expenditure compared with the original budget
● a good return on investment – compare the benefits that your organization has received against the costs incurred

- the actual time taken compared with the original schedule
- robust control procedures in place to track and monitor costs and schedules
- efficient organization so that roles and responsibilities were clearly defined
- good communication between members of the team
- the satisfaction of your customers/users and other stakeholders with the outcomes of your project.

Check the financial figures to see how actual expenditure compared with the planned expenditure in your original budget.

Acknowledge your team's work. Affirm key individuals as you thank them for their work. Celebrate your team's success in a way that is appropriate to your company or organization, inviting your project sponsor, your customers/users and other stakeholders. You could, for example, pay for a meal out for all the staff concerned and their partners.

Document lessons learnt. Identify what worked well ... and what did not go so well, and consider what measures should be taken to avoid making the same mistakes again. Such documented identification will help you on future projects. Produce a final end-of-project review and report for your project sponsor, summarizing the progress of the project, the lessons learnt and any recommendations. Ensure that these are written up. Keep your record, especially of good practice and measures to be taken to avoid making the same mistakes again.

Summary

Today, we've looked at managing a project and its various stages:

- preparing for and planning your project well, laying firm foundations as you clarify the aims and parameters and begin to assemble a project team
- working hard at costing your project in a budget, including a contingency figure to cover unexpected events
- making sure you have rigorous controls in place that monitor costs and quality as you implement the project
- putting the project into practice and completing its final stages
- evaluating your project so that you can learn lessons for next time.

Next steps

For a project you are to undertake:

1 Define its aims in 15 words.
2 Begin to work on a budget.
3 What monitoring and reporting controls do you have in place to track costs, quality and schedules?
4 Work out the hourly rate that you cost your company or organization.

Questions (answers at the back)

1. Defining project aims is:
   a) a waste of time ❑
   b) important if you can spare the time ❑
   c) nice to have ❑
   d) essential. ❑

2. A project needs:
   a) spontaneity ❑
   b) careful planning ❑
   c) no planning ❑
   d) poor motivation. ❑

3. Stakeholders are:
   a) only the users of the project ❑
   b) the team members of a project ❑
   c) all the key people involved in a project ❑
   d) the directors at lunch. ❑

4. A work breakdown structure is:
   a) a plan for when the project breaks down ❑
   b) a plan of the benefits of a project ❑
   c) a plan of the different activities in a project ❑
   d) a plan of the people needed in a project. ❑

5. When compiling a schedule, include the following:
   a) time for lunch ❑
   b) time for holidays ❑
   c) money spent on office equipment ❑
   d) staff salaries. ❑

6. Contingencies refer to:
   a) unplanned events that could significantly delay the project ❑
   b) planned events that could significantly delay the project ❑
   c) bad weather ❑
   d) good weather. ❑

7. Your project budget should be:
   a) as cool as possible ❑
   b) as futuristic as possible ❑
   c) as flexible as possible ❑
   d) as exact as possible. ❑

8. A cost centre is:
   a) a unit to which items of expenditure are allocated in a project ❑
   b) a supermarket that sells good quality food ❑
   c) a unit of profit ❑
   d) a measure of the company's overheads. ❑

9. Tracking changes involves:
   a) monitoring and reporting changes to control them ❑
   b) correcting your text ❑
   c) reporting only positive changes to the project board ❑
   d) only monitoring changes and doing nothing with your results. ❑

10. When dealing with lessons you have learnt:
   a) discuss them, but don't write them down ❑
   b) discuss them and write them down but do nothing about them ❑
   c) note them and act on them in future ❑
   d) ignore them, so that you make the same mistakes again. ❑

SATURDAY

Managing yourself

So, we're coming to the end of our week. How have you been getting on? We've looked at managing people and teams, managing work procedures, communication and projects. Perhaps the greatest challenge – even more difficult than some of those just listed – is learning to manage yourself. So in a sense, managing yourself is the key to unlocking your potential so that you can be a successful manager.

Today we will consider:

- being aware of yourself
- getting organized
- making good use of your time
- managing your boss
- coping with stress.

Each of these is important as you develop as a manager. If you don't give them any attention then you will probably still function as a manager but there will be severe limitations on your effectiveness. With them sorted, you will fulfil your potential and be successful.

Being aware of yourself

What kind of person are you? Quiet or assertive? Decisive or unsure? Confident or timid? Good at analysing words and figures or better with people? Excellent at details; not so good at the big picture – or the other way round? Highly emotional or more controlled? Good or poor at motivating others?

Ask trusted friends, but remember that you can change. My normal personality is to be quiet, retiring even, but over a period of time I made myself talk to people in social situations to the point where I am now much more confident and relaxed about meeting new people. You can change. If necessary, undertake training in areas where you need to develop: seek professional help, including a coach or mentor, for deeper guidance.

Getting organized

As a manager, you need to be organized:

● Tidy your desk. Remove clutter of paperclips, elastic bands and boxes of staples (which you probably rarely use). Put them away in a place where you can find them. Giving yourself space for your essential papers, monitor and keyboard or laptop, will give you room to think.

● If you have an in-tray and out-tray, make use of them. Sort out the papers that have stayed at the bottom of your in-tray for some time.

- Make sure your chair is well adjusted and has a foot rest.
- Arrange your computer screen at a safe and comfortable height, with the top of the screen just below eye level and at least 63 cm (about 25 inches) from your eyes.

Managing your time

Here are some tips on good time management.

Know what time of day you work best. Are you a morning person or an afternoon person? Jealously guard the time at which you work best: make sure that you use that period of time for completing tasks that require high levels of energy and creative thinking, not for doing routine administrative jobs. Don't be tempted to say, 'I'll just get these little things out of the way' at this time; instead, undertake the most challenging piece of work.

Have some form of diary: paper, electronic, digital, in the cloud – the medium doesn't matter, but the principle is vital. You need to write down (or its electronic equivalent) your tasks and appointments, what you have to do, where you have to be, who you have to email or phone.

Work out a system that functions well for you. I personally write down all my tasks (large projects, meetings, minor routine admin) on the relevant day in my A4 week-to-view diary. At the end of a day, I prepare the next day's to-do list. This used to be a straightforward list, but I now turn my A4 page to landscape orientation and list major tasks/meetings/ appointments on the left-hand side, phone calls and emails in the centre, and minor routine tasks on the right-hand side. Look at your to-do list during the day and cross off the tasks as you complete them. Work not completed one day goes onto the next day's to-do list.

Distinguish the urgent and important from the less important. Some tasks are urgent – others can wait. Plan in all important tasks. Begin now with the important and urgent.

Plan ahead. I plan major important projects on a weekly basis on a wall planner and also on the Friday before the following week. (So on Friday afternoons I plan the work for both the next week and also the following Monday.)

Be proactive; set priorities – focus on the big picture, but also don't forget to see your priorities work out practically.

Start with undertaking the tasks you don't want to do, or the largest or most difficult part of a task. As noted above, don't say to yourself, 'I'll just get these little jobs done and then I'll go on to the longer task' – that could mean you delay getting started. And if you've got only 35 minutes available for a task (before a meeting, for example) challenge yourself to fit in 45 minutes' worth of work – rather than saying to yourself, 'It's only just over half an hour – how can I manage to do much in that time?'

Put regular items in the diary. I have a major monthly planning time on a Thursday afternoon in week three of every month (Thursday, as I know I complete my creative work Monday to Wednesday; afternoon, as I complete my major thinking tasks in the morning; week three, as I have accurate figures from reconciled bank account data by that time in the month).

File clearly, whether on hard copy or digitally. Think where you are going to be able to retrieve that document from most easily. File under such directories as 'accounts', 'sales', 'invoices'. File in alphabetical or date order.

Write notes to yourself. Perhaps you think you will be able to recall a particular point, but why tax your brain with trying to remember information, particularly if it's detailed? I know I've got to proofread a book in a month's time, so I've already built up a file containing points I want to check.

Work efficiently. Group all your outgoing phone calls and respond to emails only at certain times of the day.

Deal with papers only once. Read a document then act on it or bin it. Don't keep returning to the same piece of paper: be decisive. Only file documents that are important and that you need to keep.

Get things right first time. Going over a piece of work and having to undo what went wrong earlier is a bad use of time. Not only is your work affected, but that of other colleagues and probably the perception of your customers too. Quality in your work now is vital.

Delegate work more: See **Tuesday.**

Make the most of 'slack' time, e.g. when you are waiting for the computer or printer or in a few odd minutes before a meeting. Catch up on non-urgent reading or compose a routine email during such times.

Use your computer as a computer, not just as a typewriter. One key feature I often use is 'autocorrect'. So I've stored on my computer many of the basic English words we constantly use (e.g. the, that, was, were, because, and) and have reduced them to a smaller number of keystrokes: e.g. 't' for the, 'th' for that, 'w1' for was, 'w2' for were, 'bec' for because, 'a1' for and). I did this (and with hundreds of other words too) in preparation for an 8,000,000-word book I edited over a period of six years, and I reckon it saved me two weeks' work. So if the name of your company or organization has, say, 20 keystrokes, you can type an abbreviated form. For how to use autocorrect, press F1 in Word and follow the links, or type 'autocorrect' into the Word help menu on a Mac.

Managing your boss

It may seem odd to include a section on managing your boss in a book *Introducing Management*, but you need to remember that you need to communicate not only with those who report to you but you also with your boss to whom you report.

- Find out about your boss's aims, values, challenges and style. Adapt to their style. For example, my boss prefers contact by phone rather than email, so I'm alert to that and adapt accordingly. He dislikes detail and wants the bottom line, so although I love detail, I have to follow his way.
- Communicate at the right level, usually giving more information rather than less. Keep your boss as informed as they want to be. If you can see a problem looming ahead, alert your boss as soon as possible, so that they are aware of it and can act accordingly before the matter becomes serious.
- When presenting your boss with a problem, offer a solution at the same time. This shows you have thought about it.
- Support your manager in meetings. Be loyal to them.
- Discuss priorities with your boss and make decisions with them. Discuss what they want you to do, especially if they continue to give you task after task. Agree on your goals and then, when your boss gives you an additional task, discuss with them whether that achieves the agreed goal or not. If necessary, give them the responsibility of making the decision: 'Actually, I'm working on [this project] now. What do you want me to do?' Learn to say no when necessary.

Management styles

At his interview, Carl was asked about which management style he adopted. Wisely he responded that he had several, to suit different occasions, the people he is managing and the tasks they are doing, rather than having a 'one-size-fits-all' approach.

So he said that at times his style is democratic, involving the whole team in the decision-making process. He uses this especially in change-management situations when he wants the team to be committed to change. At other times, particularly when dealing with very urgent matters, he is directional and simply has to tell people what to do

> ('The customer has changed his mind and wants new figures by 3.00 p.m. today'). That wasn't his preferred style, however, he added, wanting to give responsibility to his team members, together with training, support and clear instructions and trusting them to get on with the tasks using their own good judgment.

Coping with stress

We're coming to the end of our week on *Introducing Management* and you may be feeling a little overwhelmed: managing people, teams, policies and procedures, projects ... good communication is vital, as is the ability to manage yourself. How can you avoid getting stressed out by it all?

Acknowledge that stress will come. In fact, a little stress may be good for you, but if it gets out of control it can become a problem. You may know the particular ways in which stress may affect you personally. Plan for it, even though you won't know when it may strike:

- Build in regular times off. Don't overfill every moment of your 24 hours. For example, if you're busy for two weeks, make sure in week 3 you have some slack 'me' time.
- Build in regular patterns of exercise and breaks. Join a gym; play sport. During the first few years of my working life I

pushed myself too hard and had to learn to relax. So now I make myself take regular walks. However brief, physical exercise helps. I find the occasional walk in a nearby park at lunch helps particularly.

- Eat and drink sensibly. You know the rules – apply them! You can't remain healthy in the long term on a diet of junk food, and drinking and smoking excessively.
- Have a life outside work – yes, really! Spend time with your partner, family, friends. Join a club. Take up a hobby. Take holidays without feeling guilty ... and without all your electronic gadgets! Take up other activities and be reminded what it is to be human.

If it all gets too much:

- Visit your GP.
- Switch off the TV or computer earlier and get more sleep.
- Discuss matters with your boss. Can you be relieved of some areas of work? Can some activities be delayed? Delegate more!
- Focus on what you can do – a little is better than nothing.
- Learn relaxation techniques for your body – even simple deep-breathing techniques can work wonders. Focus on the positive in your mind.

Saying no

Bob felt flattered to be asked to join a committee to look at succession planning, but he wasn't sure about it. He felt he was already fully stretched and that a further commitment might just be too much. Bob had lunch with Mike, the chairman, who told him about the responsibilities, but Bob said no at that time. Bob added that he thought it likely his other commitments would lessen six months later when he was due to have an assistant who could cover some of his responsibilities. Sure enough, six months later, Mike asked Bob again and then, with some fresh capacity because he had the assistant, Bob accepted the offer.

Summary

I wish you well with your role as manager. You will have successes ... and probably a few failures. (Remember, 'the person who never made mistakes never made anything'.) The main thing is that you will learn about how to get the best out of other people – how to motivate them, how to inspire them – and how to get the best out of yourself.

Soon you will have mastered everything in this short book and be ready for further promotion as your career progresses. Remember, go for quality: it's all very well dreaming about the future, but do a good job with the task in hand now.

Next steps

1 What are your strengths and weaknesses? What can you change?
2 What is the next step in your company or organization? What do you want to talk over with your coach or mentor?
3 What courses could you go on for training in specific areas (e.g. new software, time management) and wider areas like leadership?
4 How could you be better organized?
5 Think of three ways in which you can make better use of your time. Plan them into your diary for next week now.
6 Work on changing your lifestyle and work patterns to help you cope with stress.

Questions (answers at the back)

1. Being organized as a manager is:
   a) a nice-to-have ❑
   b) unimportant ❑
   c) essential ❑
   d) I'm too laid back to answer. ❑

2. As a manager, having a diary or some form of recording work and appointments is:
   a) essential ❑
   b) nice to have ❑
   c) unimportant ❑
   d) I haven't got the time to answer. ❑

3. Always complete the important tasks before the tasks that are urgent.
   a) True ❑
   b) I'm not sure. ❑
   c) I don't care. ❑
   d) False ❑

4. Complete all the small tasks before tackling the major ones.
   a) False ❑
   b) True ❑
   c) I'm not sure. ❑
   d) I don't care. ❑

5. Forward planning is:
   a) a luxury ❑
   b) I haven't got the time to answer. ❑
   c) a waste of time ❑
   d) essential ❑

6. Spending time thinking how and where to file documents is:
   a) I haven't got the time to answer. ❑
   b) essential ❑

   c) a nice-to-have ❑
   d) a waste of time ❑

7. When I present my boss with a problem:
   a) I leave them to come up with a solution. ❑
   b) I don't trust them to solve it. ❑
   c) I also come up with a solution. ❑
   d) I never see my boss. ❑

8. I know what days of the week and what time of day I work best and so:
   a) I treat that time like any other period of time. ❑
   b) I do my best to guard and reserve that time for quality work. ❑
   c) I fill that time with small routine tasks. ❑
   d) I go home at such times. ❑

9. When I'm asked to take on another task:
   a) I never say 'No'. ❑
   b) I always say 'No'. ❑
   c) I always say 'Yes'. ❑
   d) I sometimes say 'No', asking if it is part of my job. ❑

10. When seeking to avoid stress:
    a) I never get stressed. ❑
    b) I'm always stressed anyway. ❑
    c) I plan my lifestyle to cope with it. ❑
    d) I hope I don't get stressed. ❑

Survivng in tough times

Organizations that value their employees create a culture which enables the employees not only to survive in but also to adapt to tough economic times. As a manager, your role in making that success a reality is critical. As well as being the support for the team below you, you are also the channel for passing information from higher in the organization.

1 Value your team

Value your colleagues *as a team*, with yourself as one person in that group. Consider not only the day-to-day minutiae of your colleagues' jobs but also their broader roles within the team – look back at Belbin's nine team roles (**Tuesday**). Be genuine in listening to, and motivating, your colleagues.

2 Encourage good teamwork

You are the team leader. It is your responsibility to get the best out of your colleagues. Communicate a strong and inspiring vision for your team (see **Tuesday**). Where is the team going? What is its core purpose? In uncertain economic times morale can be low, so draw attention to success whenever you can. Lead by example in your dealings with team members. Be fair and treat all your colleagues equally, even though you may like some more than others.

3 Be clear about your goals

Your team vision needs to be expressed in practical steps. Really know your objectives and express them clearly. All goals should be SMART – specific, measurable, agreed, realistic, rimed (see **Monday**) – but this is all the more true in difficult times. An uncertain economic environment is unforgiving of vagueness at all levels of a business enterprise. Make your team count.

4 Manage your systems efficiently

Take a step back and objectively consider your managerial systems, e.g. for setting and managing budgets (see **Wednesday**). Now may not be the time to install a new IT system, but you can probably find more efficient ways of working in some areas. What procedures can you streamline? Work at making your team undertake tasks more effectively – this should free up more of your own time for problem solving and making decisions, which should be your priorities.

5 Make informed decisions

Concentrate on solving problems creatively, knowing that mistakes will cost money. Stay informed of what is happening in your wider organization and in the industry as a whole. If your boss's aims and challenges are changing, this will obviously impact on you and your team. Consider your management style (see **Saturday**) and whether this needs to change if members of your team are facing difficult circumstances.

6 Improve communications

When things get tough and colleagues become stressed, you need to be even more certain that you are getting your message across well. Keep lines of communication open to avoid misunderstandings. If you are able to have regular one-to-one meetings with your team, so much the better.

Keep focused both on the medium and long term by continuing to plan ahead, and on the short term by working on your listening skills (**Thursday**) and keeping on top of your email inbox. Be open, honest and consistent in your dealings and others will do the same for you.

7 Delegate

As a manager, you need to focus on the big issues. Working yourself into the ground is not going to solve anything, and is just as likely to be counterproductive. As discussed on **Tuesday**, delegate: to colleagues who are 'nearly ready', whole tasks wherever possible, having completed thorough planning. Supervise the delegated task, and offer yourself for problem solving, but do let it go. Remember to express your appreciation of your colleague(s) when the task is completed.

8 Plan better meetings

If you ever find yourself in a meeting thinking, 'What is the point of this?' (or suspect this in others), it's time to make some changes. Effort put into preparation and follow up will be well rewarded. Look back at the notes on chairing a meeting (**Thursday**) and ensure that you lead the way by participating fully yourself. Consider the possibility of having fewer meetings.

9 Improve your project management

Think ahead when managing a project. Don't assume that everyone is clear about their responsibilities – make sure they are. If necessary, produce a scope of work (see**Friday**), particularly for outside suppliers. Work out – and keep to – your aims, outputs, costs and schedules. As manager, your monitoring systems are key to spotting looming problems; your aim should then be to deal with these firmly and speedily. Above all, learn from experience.

10 Take steps to manage yourself

If you have not already done so, work out the hourly rate which you personally cost your company (see **Friday**). You may not be able to create an economy-busting strategy for your employer, but you can – and should – aim to save them money by being more efficient with your time. Organize yourself. Plan ahead. Compose emails thoughtfully. Get things – even small things – right first time, knowing that going back over them later is inefficient and costly. Remember to be positive about what you have achieved as well as looking to everything that still needs to be completed.

Answers

Sunday: 1c; 2d; 3b; 4b; 5a; 6c; 7d; 8a; 9c; 10d

Monday: 1d; 2c; 3b; 4b; 5a; 6c; 7b; 8b; 9b; 10d

Tuesday: 1c; 2b; 3a; 4d; 5b; 6b; 7c; 8a; 9d; 10c

Wednesday: 1c; 2d; 3c; 4b; 5a; 6d; 7c; 8b; 9a; 10b

Thursday: 1b; 2b; 3c; 4c; 5d; 6c; 7b; 8a; 9d; 10b

Friday: 1d; 2b; 3c; 4c; 5b; 6a; 7d; 8a; 9a; 10c

Saturday: 1c; 2a; 3d; 4a; 5d, 6b; 7c; 8b; 9d; 10c

ALSO AVAILABLE IN THE 'IN A WEEK' SERIES

BODY LANGUAGE FOR MANAGEMENT • BOOKKEEPING AND ACCOUNTING • CUSTOMER CARE • SPEED READING • DEALING WITH DIFFICULT PEOPLE • EMOTIONAL INTELLIGENCE • FINANCE FOR NON-FINANCIAL MANAGERS • INTRODUCING MANAGEMENT • MANAGING YOUR BOSS • MARKET RESEARCH • NEURO-LINGUISTIC PROGRAMMING • OUTSTANDING CREATIVITY • PLANNING YOUR CAREER • SUCCEEDING AT INTERVIEWS • SUCCESSFUL APPRAISALS • SUCCESSFUL ASSERTIVENESS • SUCCESSFUL BUSINESS PLANS • SUCCESSFUL CHANGE MANAGEMENT • SUCCESSFUL COACHING • SUCCESSFUL COPYWRITING • SUCCESSFUL CVS • SUCCESSFUL INTERVIEWING

SUCCES...
COPYWR...

Sunday: Sunday – work out what you want to say Monday: put yourself in your readers' shoes Tuesday: learn the art of letter writing Wednesday: understand advertising Thursday: become a popular press commentator Friday: discover why most promotional print says noth... Saturday: explore some of words

LEARN IN A WEE...
WHAT THE LEAD...
LEARN IN A LIFE...

ROBERT ASHTON
LEADING EXPERT AN...

Teach Yourself

SUCCESSFUL NEGOTIATIN...

Sunday: Learn how to set up the best "environment" for a negotiation Monday: know how to research and plan your objectives Tuesday:Consider variations in the venue of a meeting Wednesday: Explore the opening me... the meeting Thursday: ... the best ways of moving ... negotiation forward Frida... negotiation to a satisfactory... how you can continue to grow... skills

LEARN IN A WEEK,
WHAT THE LEADING EXPERTS
LEARN IN A LIFETIME

PETER FLEMING
LEADING EXPERT AND TRAINER

IN A WEEK

For information about other titles in the series, please visit www.inaweek.co.uk

ALSO AVAILABLE IN THE 'IN A WEEK' SERIES

For information about other titles in the series, please visit www.inaweek.co.uk

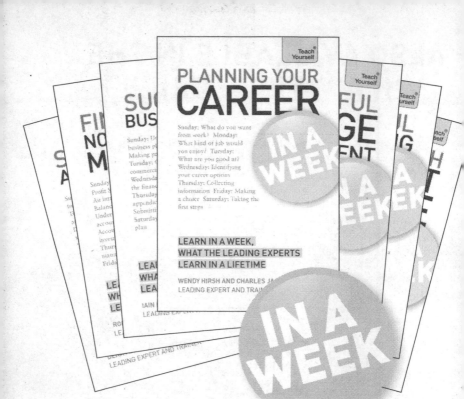